CHANGE
The Independent Group

Edited and Compiled by
Peter McNab

Grosvenor House
Publishing Limited

The right of Ann Coffey to be identified as the author of this
work has been asserted in accordance with Section 78
of the Copyright, Designs and Patents Act 1988

This book is published by
Grosvenor House Publishing Ltd
Link House
140 The Broadway, Tolworth, Surrey, KT6 7HT.
www.grosvenorhousepublishing.co.uk

A CIP record for this book
is available from the British Library

ISBN 978-1-83975-465-4

CONTENTS

INTRODUCTION

This book is based on many hours of recorded interviews and discussions with the five former Change UK MPs who were left just before the party was dissolved – Ann Coffey, Anna Soubry, Chris Leslie, Joan Ryan and Mike Gapes. Apart from editing and rearranging the content (and the linking commentary in bold), what follows is entirely in their own words.

On Monday 18 February 2019, seven Labour MPs announced that they were leaving the party with the following statement:

The Independent Group of MPs

Each of us has dedicated decades to the progressive values that were once held true by Labour, values which have since been abandoned by today's Labour Party.

Labour now pursues policies that would weaken our national security; accepts the narratives of states hostile to our country; has failed to take a lead in addressing the challenge of Brexit and to provide a strong and coherent alternative to the Conservatives' approach; is passive in circumstances of international humanitarian distress; is hostile to businesses large and small; and threatens to destabilise the British economy in pursuit of ideological objectives.

For a Party that once committed to pursue a spirit of solidarity, tolerance and respect, it has changed beyond recognition. Today, visceral hatreds of other people, views and opinions are commonplace in and around the Labour Party.

It is not simply that our values are no longer welcome in the Labour Party; the values we hold mean that, in all conscience, we can have no confidence in the Party's collective leadership, competence or culture.

To fix our broken politics, we are clear that we want to develop a different approach. We recognise that every member of our group has the right to be heard and a duty to lead ...

Sitting as the Independent Group of MPs we appeal to colleagues from all parties to consider the best interests of the country above short-term party-political considerations and choose to do likewise.

At the same time, they issued a set of 11 values that they had developed over several months and that would be the basis of what would become their new party:

Our values

We believe –

Ours is a great country of which people are rightly proud, where the first duty of government must be to defend its people and do whatever it takes to safeguard Britain's national security.

Britain works best as a diverse, mixed social market economy, in which well-regulated private enterprise can reward aspiration and drive economic progress and where government has the responsibility to ensure the sound stewardship of taxpayer's money and a stable, fair and balanced economy.

A strong economy means we can invest in our public services. We believe the collective provision of public services and the NHS can be delivered through government action, improving health and educational life chances, protecting the public, safeguarding the vulnerable, ensuring dignity at every stage of life and placing individuals at the heart of decision-making.

The people of this country have the ability to create fairer, more prosperous communities for present and future generations. We believe that this creativity is best realised in a society which fosters individual freedom and supports all families.

The barriers of poverty, prejudice and discrimination facing individuals should be removed and advancement occur on the basis of merit, with inequalities reduced through the extension of opportunity, giving individuals the skills and means to open new doors and fulfil their ambitions.

Individuals are capable of taking responsibility if opportunities are offered to them, everybody can and should make a contribution to society and that contribution should be recognised. Paid work should be secure and pay should be fair.

Our free media, the rule of law, and our open, tolerant and respectful democratic society should be cherished and renewed.

We believe that our parliamentary democracy in which our elected representatives deliberate, decide and provide leadership, held accountable by their whole electorate is the best system of representing the views of the British people.

In order to face the challenges and opportunities presented by globalisation, migration and technological advances, we believe the multilateral, international rules-based order must be strengthened and reformed. We believe in maintaining strong alliances with our closest European and international allies on trade, regulation, defence, security and counterterrorism.

As part of the global community, we have a responsibility to future generations to protect our environment, safeguard the planet, plan development sustainably and to act on the urgency of climate change.

Power should be devolved to the most appropriate level, trusting and involving local communities. More powers and representation should be given to local government to act in the best interests of their communities.

On Tuesday 19 February 2019 they were joined by Joan Ryan who resigned from the Labour Party in support of the Jewish community.

They were joined by three Conservative MPs on 20 February 2019.

Although they did not achieve their aspiration: a new party that would lead a change in British politics, they did show that there was a huge appetite for change; people were looking for something new, something different. There was a significant response in the early days and over 100,000 people with remarkably diverse views signed up on the new group's website, and at one point they were as high as 18% in the polls (according to YouGov). Followers on Twitter exceeded Momentum's, with around 130,000, and 3,500 people applied to be MEP candidates at the European election. There was a real groundswell of interest during that initial phase.

That appetite is still there, and the opportunity to create change is still there. The difficulties of doing that through creating a new parliamentary party are evident in this account. The challenge is how to express that desire for change through policies and ideas that bring people together in a reaffirmation of a social consensus; that, of course, is the challenge that faces democracies in the US and in the UK. "Change" showed the problems but also the appetite for something "different", and that reaffirms optimism and hope and shows us that there is a way forward that is built on consent not division, together.

But it has to start with people.

The 5 MPs wanted to put on record their personal experience, why they felt they had to leave the party and what they wanted to achieve. They are very different people with different histories, personal experiences, personalities and interests but what they have in common was the desire to make politics different and the willingness to show that commitment by resigning from their party and entering a political wilderness.

I have really enjoyed getting to know all five of them and how and why they responded to the political situation that they found themselves in after decades of public service. I discovered that what they all have in common is that their actions were spurred by their principles, and in most cases these principles developed during childhood; so, agree with their behaviours or not, one cannot argue that these did not come from integrity. Something that emerged, independently, was the question of whether or not they could look themselves in the mirror each morning.

Several themes emerged as I was editing this book:

- Why would anyone choose to go into politics and even make it a lifelong career? One of the popular myths is that people go into politics for power and prestige and fame; this proved not to be the case.
- Why did five totally committed Party MPs leave the political party of which they had been members for decades and set up what became The Independent Group for Change?
- Where do the personal and the political meet?
- Can politics be "fixed"?

It might be useful to have some background and contextualising:

In 1992, the Labour Party under Neil Kinnock lost the general election, and John Major remained Conservative Prime Minister. In that same election, Ann Coffey was first elected as Labour MP for Stockport, and Mike Gapes for Ilford South. Two years later, John Smith died, and Tony Blair became the Labour Party leader. He led the Labour Party into its landslide victory of 1997. Ann Coffey and Mike Gapes were re-elected, and Joan Ryan joined them in Parliament as Labour MP for Enfield North. Chris Leslie was also elected for Labour for Shipley and the youngest MP in the country at 24. The 2001 general election was also a decisive win for Blair and our four MPs were re-elected again. 2005 was another win for Labour and Ann Coffey, Mike Gapes and Joan Ryan kept their seats again, but Chris Leslie lost his seat that year. Tony Blair stood down as Prime Minister two years later to be succeeded by Gordon Brown.

After 13 years in power, Labour lost the 2010 general election, and Conservative David Cameron formed a coalition with the Liberal Democrat leader Nick Clegg. Ann Coffey and Mike Gapes were again elected, but Joan Ryan lost her seat in Enfield North. At the same time, Chris Leslie was elected as Labour MP for Nottingham East and Anna Soubry as Conservative MP for Broxtowe. In the aftermath of the election, Gordon Brown stepped down as leader of the Labour Party and Ed Miliband was elected in his stead. In 2014, Scotland voted by 55% to 45% to reject Independence.

In the 2015 general election, David Cameron led the Conservatives to an overall majority and the Liberal Democrats crashed. Ann Coffey, Anna Soubry, Chris Leslie, and Mike Gapes were all re-elected, while Joan Ryan regained Enfield North. Shortly after this, Ed Miliband resigned as Labour leader and Jeremy Corbyn was elected as Labour leader, which is where our story really begins.

While I am not superstitious, I sometimes find coincidences a bit spooky. On 29 October 2020 at 10.00am, the Equality and Human Rights Commission released their report, *Investigation into antisemitism in the Labour Party*, in which they find that the Labour Party acted unlawfully over the issue of anti-Semitism.

The Foreword states that *"trust should be at the heart of a political party's relationship with its members, and with the wider general public; yet what this investigation has shown is a clear breakdown of trust between the Labour Party, many of its members and the Jewish community ... We found specific examples of harassment, discrimination and political interference in our evidence, but equally of concern was a lack of leadership within the Labour Party on these issues, which is hard to reconcile with its stated commitment to a zero-tolerance approach to antisemitism."*

According to the BBC, at 10.36, Jeremy Corbyn stated that although there was a problem, it was *"dramatically overstated"*. Just over half an hour later, Keir Starmer was reported as saying that anyone who thinks that the problem is *"exaggerated or a factional attack ... [is] part of the problem."* At 12.15 Jeremy Corbyn recorded an interview that was broadcast 45 minutes later where he repeated that cases were exaggerated in the report and that he disagreed with various parts of the report. Six minutes later the Labour Party suspended Jeremy Corbyn.

As you will read, the issue of anti-Semitism played a large part in the reasons why the four Labour Party MPs left the party of which they had been members for decades.

The story starts in 2015, but first we shall meet the five MPs with a total of 97 years of experience in Parliament, and who had been members of their respective political parties for 205 years. It's time to find out who these people are, some of their history, and some of their accomplishments.

Peter McNab
January 2021
Rossendale

CHAPTER ONE

Biographies – *"The Personal is Political"*

Ann Coffey, MP for Stockport, 1992–2019

Ann Coffey with her mum on an election night in Stockport

My father was born in Queensferry, which is just outside Edinburgh; one of eight children, his father worked on the boats that went between North and South Queensferry; he shovelled coal on the ferry, and it was a very hard life for the parents and the children. When the war came, like many young men, my father joined up and went into the Air Force. He was very lucky to survive the war and he stayed on in the Air Force after the war because that offered him a career opportunity. My mother was also a Scot who came from a farming family. Her father worked as a farm labourer, and that was also a hard life. Her sister died of TB at the age of 16, and I do not think my grandmother ever recovered from that. My mother took the opportunity to train as a nurse during the war. My parents were both very proud that they "had got on". My father voted Conservative when he could. He saw the party as supporting people like himself who wanted to "get on". He died before I was elected, I think he would have thought I had "got on".

My school career was somewhat interrupted because we moved every two years, because the RAF move people to a different base every two years. So, I went to a number of different primary schools and secondary schools. It was a bit of a problem sometimes particularly if the new curriculum was totally different to the one in my previous school. I became interested in politics when I was at Bushey Grammar School and I remember watching the hustings in Watford in the 1964 election. My politics didn't go down well with my father nor my conversion to nuclear disarmament.

I took advantage of Harold Wilson's expansion of the polytechnics to do a degree in sociology at the then Borough Polytechnic in 1966. I was Vice-President of the Students Union. One of our early campaigns was protesting against the imposition of fees for overseas students. One of my first jobs was as a computer programmer. I don't think I appreciated the impact this new technology would have on all our lives.

However, I wasn't very good at programming and wanted to do something that was more concerned with people. I went on to train, first, as a teacher in Walsall, and then as a social worker in Manchester. I did a further degree, an MSc in Psychiatric Social Work, at Manchester University. I worked with children and families until my election as the Member of Parliament for Stockport in 1992

One of my first adjournment debates in the House of Commons was on children's homes and that was an interest I continued to follow for the next 27 years of my time as an MP. I moved to Stockport in 1977 and joined the Labour Party in 1978. Stockport has been an important part of my life. My daughter went to school there, I was a local councillor before becoming the MP. One of the reasons it was extremely hard to leave the Labour Party was because I was cutting off my political and personal relationships with people in Stockport who I had worked and campaigned with for over 40 years.

I've had a very interesting Parliamentary career, and particularly the years the Labour Party was in power; I was Tony Blair's Parliamentary Private Secretary, and then Alistair Darling's PPS while he was Chancellor of the Exchequer at the time of the crash of 2008. Alistair's book *Back from the Brink* has been described as 'a heck of a good read' of the events of time he was Chancellor. And I was privileged to sit in on some remarkably interesting meetings. Alistair was a well-respected minister by officials in all the departments he led and by MPs on all sides of the House of Commons because he took difficult decisions in the public interest and had integrity.

The role of a PPS is to make sure that the minister understands the views of backbenchers, because when views are not listened to, things can go very badly wrong, particularly when it requires a vote in the House of Commons. Sometimes even listening doesn't stop public rows and votes lost. It's trying to get that understanding, and keeping the communication going that is the key to supporting the minister and the government. Backbenchers need access to ministers and Alistair was always willing to meet and talk. It is also important that an MP's constituents can see they are doing their job, by representing their views to ministers.

When the Labour Party was no longer in government, I turned my attention to campaigns. I became the Chair of the All-Party Group on Runaway and Missing Children and Adults in 2010.

I had excellent staff in both the Stockport and the London office. The APPG was supported in their work by the charities, Missing People, and The Children's Society. We produced several reports, over the years, identifying the link between children going missing and their vulnerability to exploitation. Initially that exploitation of children was sexual, but we soon became concerned, about the criminal exploitation of children, as more and more evidence became available of how organised drug gangs were using vulnerable children to transport and supply drugs to towns and villages, outside the metropolitan areas, where they saw the opportunities for new markets. We also took an interest in the structure of the children's home market. There was very little choice for local councils of where to place children, because most of the children's homes were in the either North West or the West Midlands. This meant that children from other areas were placed at a distance from their local area where there were vacancies. Sometimes the placement was hundreds of miles away from their home. This made them more vulnerable. They were vulnerable anyway because of mental health issue, poor family relationships and histories of exclusion from schools. Many had multiple placements. They were being placed somewhere where they had no support, out of communities they knew, away from friends they might have had, away from any contacts, and from familiar places.

The reasons for this were not because those placements met the needs of those children, although sometimes that was the reason given, it was simply the structure of the children's homes market and where the providers (70% of whom are in the private sector) of children's homes decided it was in their best business interests to register homes. Local councils' direct provision had steadily declined since the 1990s.

It is in fact a market in which the commodity is children.

The All-Party Parliamentary Group on Runaway and Missing Children and Adults also did some good reports on the need for better inter-agency working between Health and the Police to give early help to those adults most at risk when they go missing.

I also enjoyed writing two independent reports for the then Police and Crime Commissioner for Greater Manchester, Tony Lloyd MP. In 2014, he asked me to make an observation as to whether the situation had improved in Greater Manchester since the Rochdale grooming scandal in 2012 when there had been a shaming failure to respond to sexually exploited children who were blamed for their own sexual abuse. The report *Real Voices* was published in October 2014. I did a follow-up report in March 2017 *Real Voices – Are they being heard?* The point that I made in those reports, and continued to make over the years, was fundamentally that the problem was and is our attitude as a society to children.

Children who had been sexually exploited were described in the Rochdale trials and, indeed, by children's safeguarding agencies as "child prostitutes". The description a "child prostitute" means there's a transaction taking place. How can an immature child protected in law 'choose' such a transaction? Exploitation is not a choice. Child means a child, a child is immature, a child because of that immaturity is given special protection in law.

Adults have to take responsibility for the relationships they have with children, not the children themselves.

To give Theresa May her credit, she was good on this issue, and in 2015, after some lobbying, Parliament changed the law, so that we wiped out the phrase "child prostitution" from all existing statutes. Wherever you look you will no longer see the term "child prostitution" anymore, but rather, "sexually exploited child". How you describe behaviour, dictates how you see it. If we are going to really eradicate this problem of the exploitation of children, a starting point is recognising the power of language, so that we have a better and more responsible attitude to children. We must stop blaming them for the relationships that we have with them; it's our responsibility as adults and not theirs.

This Real Voices report in 2014 got a lot of publicity. Joy Copley, who worked for me for a number of years was really excellent; she had previously been a journalist and was very good at getting media interest in our reports. Publicity does change attitudes and is very, very, important. The last report that the All-Party Group for Runaway and Missing Children and Adults published, *No Place at Home,* was in September 2019. It was an inquiry into children going missing from out of area care placements. It included children placed in unregulated settings. *Newsnight* did a series of documentaries on the topic to which there were a number of contributors including young people themselves. It was very powerful. The government responded positively and launched a consultation over changes in regulation.

Anna Soubry, MP for Broxtowe, 2010–2019

Anna Soubry campaigning in 2019 at a Remain rally

My mother worked pretty much all her life in Doncaster. In the 1960s, she came across a young doctor who had come over from Uganda; he was one of the people who were kicked out by Idi Amin. His origins were Asian, and he didn't know anybody in Doncaster and my mother befriended him and thought nothing of it. At the time there was hardly anybody in Worksop who wasn't white. She just thought, "Well, that's what you do, you look after somebody and you befriend them, because it must be quite scary for them having been thrown out of their country and not knowing anybody." The fact that he had brown skin didn't matter to her; at that time, where we were, I think that was quite unusual. My mother knew somebody who was gay, and it was like, "Yeah, so what?" kind of thing. "Doesn't really matter. Got a problem with that?" "No." I think that they were small "l" liberals. So, growing up I was surrounded by tolerance; that was quite a feature of my upbringing, plus that sense that you did the right thing, you should do the right thing, I think that was just there.

My father always said, "You should be able to look yourself in the mirror." I always remember that; my father saying that. Men tend to shave every morning, and he said, "Every morning when I have a shave, I think, I don't want to be ashamed of the person looking back at me; I want to be at ease with the person looking back at me in the mirror."

That stuck with me a lot, and through all of the Brexit stuff, I can't tell you how strong that was as an influence. That thought got me through some very, very, very difficult and unpleasant times. I believe that you've got to do what you believe is right.

I think it's important to say that I joined the Conservative Party as a student back in 1975 or 1976, when I was about 20 years of age. I was active in student politics, and the only Conservative on the NUS Executive. At that time, I was very much involved in politics.

When I was a student involved in politics, I learnt something about myself, that I've got a peculiar mind; I've got a semi-photographic memory; I'm one of those people who has to see things in my head to understand something. For everything I think about conjures up a picture. When I was a student, I felt this disconnect, there we were sitting, talking, in esoteric ways, formulating policy and being terribly clever; the same thing when I was a minister. All I ever thought about was, "What does that mean for the real person in the real world?

How does that impact on that real person?" I could almost see that person living their life, being that student, when I was involved in student politics and that policy, how did it impact on that individual student?"

I took that all the way through, when I came back into politics, and then went into government. I'd sit there and they'd talk, I'd sit in these rooms and all these fucking inter-ministerial groups and they have all this whiffle-waffle, and it's often very clever, brilliant brains, talking about things. For me, it was, "Yeah, yeah, but I'm trying to see, how does that impact on this person that I'm imagining who's running a business and they're trying to deal with all this? How does this – in the real world, how is that working?" This means that I'm extremely annoying because I would say, "Sorry, I don't understand what that means and how does that work for that real person?" A lot of people be they civil servants, or politicians, or think tank people, they just don't see it in that way. They see it in a slightly more intellectualised way, but not actually the nub of it, the reality; how does that impact on real people?

In the early 1980s, I left the Conservative Party quite publicly, because at that time I felt that the Thatcher government was embarking on a right-wing agenda that I just did not subscribe to; I believed that it was going in the wrong direction. The SDP had been formed, but I decided not to join them. This is important to me because it shows what I believe in and have always believed in. My political beliefs are important to me and I am not afraid of saying, "I'm sorry, but I don't want to be involved in this thing anymore, because I don't feel at home here, I don't feel comfortable here." When I left, I'd started to get fed up with politics anyway; I lived, ate, drank, and slept politics and I wanted out of it. I wanted to have a proper life, a real life and not a political one; I also had no political ambitions.

I had started a job that took me into broadcasting, which meant that I couldn't be a member of a political party. It was time to move on in my life, and that is what I did. I think that this is important as I then spent the next thirty-odd years actually getting a life, having a real life, and doing the jobs that I did.

In the 2000s, I looked at the state of the Conservative Party and I just despaired at it. Iain Duncan Smith was elected leader. It was a right-wing rump, and it was dreadful. Why would you want to join it? At that time, I working as a criminal barrister and seeing injustices and the things that happen in the real world which I didn't think the Blair government was addressing properly. I moaned an awful lot and my friends, quite rightly, said, "Oh, shut up moaning, if you feel so strongly, you should get involved." And then, I heard somebody on the radio, on the *Today Programme*, talking about the link between drugs and crime and felt that they were making what I knew was a very good point, the right point: if we get people off drugs, it will have an impact on a large number of offences, which touch the lives of real people, acquisitive offences, notably, street robberies and house burglaries. I remember this interview very clearly and at the conclusion I thought, I don't know who that is, but whoever it is, my God, he's talking sense, and it was Oliver Letwin. He was the Shadow Home Secretary at the time. I thought, "Right, I've had enough of this, I'm going to re-join the Conservative Party," which I did.

In 2005, under Michael Howard's leadership, I stood for Parliament. Later that year, David Cameron became leader. My conservatism was very much of the Ken Clarke kind, pragmatic, slightly paternalistic, more social democratic, certainly liberal with a small "l", conservatism. I supported Ken in the leadership election and when he fell out of the election, I backed Cameron. I finally got elected in 2010.

I liked a lot of what was happening with Cameron. I liked the coalition with the Lib Dems, and the collaboration, working with people, and not the usual tribal nonsenses.

In 2010, I was elected to Parliament, and that same year within three or four months I was appointed as a PPS. I was pleased to serve in the coalition government and enjoyed the work. I never had a problem with working with the Lib Dems, because I liked the Liberal MPs that I worked with. In my opinion, there was a big difference between the MPs and a lot of local activists, because in my experience they're a very different kettle of fish. I had no problem with people like David Laws, people like Nick Clegg. I had a lot of time for Nick Clegg, Jo Swinson, Norman Lamb and others. Working cross-party was not a problem and did not trouble me. There were occasions when you would vote in the same lobby as the Labour Party, and same-sex marriage would be a very good example of that. You have to remember that the majority of Conservative MPs voted against equal marriage, so there were occasions like that when you were in the same lobby as Labour sensibles, because the Labour Party supported it.

I distinctly remember being in those voting lobbies, which are not pleasant places, because they're rammed full of people; they usually smell of sewage, stale bodies, and God knows what else. I remember looking at people in the lobby of my own party and thinking, "I genuinely do not know what I have in common with him" (it usually was with him, usually hims), and that sat with me quite uneasily. You work with your local party members and mostly I was in despair, thinking, "I just don't know what I really have in common with you, and I don't know why you're involved in politics." The seeds of worry were certainly there from early on, and there were some sprouts coming from those seeds; there was some germination going on even under Cameron's leadership.

My proudest moment as a minister was when I was in Health, and we got plain packaging on cigarettes. We made a big difference around cigarettes and tackling smoking. While in Defence, undoubtedly, it was changing the law, and the longstanding injustice for widows who, if they remarried, lost their pension. Without being too big-headed, I came up with the argument. The government wanted to do it, but they couldn't think of an argument. I came up with it, gave it to my Secretary of State, Michael Fallon, who took it to Number 10 and persuaded Cameron to do it. We did it, so, that was a great one. In Business, it was getting the support package for Redcar, and saving Port Talbot steel works as well. At one point I actually was that person that said, "I think we should buy it for a quid." But it never came to that. We saved Scunthorpe, and we saved Port Talbot, but we couldn't save Redcar, but at least we put the recovery money in there. I was only there for just over a year.

When I got re-elected in 2017, I thought, I need now to make sure I can look back at my time in Broxtowe and say, "Ah, I did that, and I did that." As a big fan of HS2, I'd like to think I was part of helping to make the case for HS2 to come to a part of Broxtowe. I mean, I couldn't claim all that, but making sure it was done right, that would've been a nice legacy to have had in 2022, to say, "Well, that's it." And at least I've put down the foundations for HS2 to be done properly in Broxtowe. And there were some other little bits and bobs.

Chris Leslie, MP for Shipley, 1997–2005 and MP for Nottingham East, 2010–2019

Chris Leslie talking to a meeting of supporters in Nottingham in April 2019 as part of a series of rallies across the country

Both my parents worked in the public services, my father, an architect with Bradford Council and my mother, a lecturer at Shipley College. So, I grew up hearing stories of what was happening in the Thatcher years to teaching, housing, public facilities and other cherished community services demoted in an era of rampant individualism. I attended our local state comprehensive school, Bingley Grammar, and was clearly politicised from the outset; our classroom ceilings were literally crumbling onto our heads and when I heard that the then Secretary of State for Education, Kenneth Baker, was visiting Bradford, I found a way to take some 'time off' and observed his city centre walkabout with the local press.

I decided it would be worth walking alongside for a while and, after he passed through the BHS store, I managed to stand in front of him – quite confident for a teenager! – and said, "My school roof is held up with chicken wire to stop it falling on our heads; what are you going to do about that?!" Looking back, it must have been quite a strange thing for him to encounter! He tried to answer about funding investment, but it was when he pushed on and his entourage elbowed past me that I thought I really should try and get into this politics business and change things for the better.

So, my motives to get involved were partly from family background and partly from my own experiences. I joined the local Labour Party in Bingley and got involved in many local campaigns, elected as Youth Officer at Shipley CLP then observing Bradford Labour Group and spending time helping the then leader Tommy Flanagan in the run up to the 1992 general election.

My degree at Leeds University – surprise, surprise – was in Politics and Parliamentary Studies, which included the third year, half in Washington DC interning in Congress, and half in Westminster working for an MP. A brilliant course which gave real political experience on my CV. As my mother was American with my grandmother living in Vermont, I ended up working for the then Congressman Bernie Sanders, which will probably surprise quite a few on the left! But Bernie was an American progressive, not an anti-west Marxist, who understood the importance of national security, didn't for a minute entertain anti-Semitism and who loved his country. I learned a lot working in his office. In Westminster I worked for Gordon Brown, then the Shadow Chancellor of the Exchequer in 1 Parliament Street, who had an adjoining office with Tony Blair when he was Shadow Home Secretary. That was an amazing formative time, the birth of 'New Labour' and while John Smith was leader.

Looking back, my political outlook was clearly influenced by my close affinity with those key figures in the early New Labour years; a determination to convince the mainstream breadth of the public that progressive values could be trusted and competent in government; helping Gordon Brown dispel the notion that Labour invariably wasted taxpayers' money by identifying resources to match spending pledges; and for family background reasons and having seen Congress in action including campaigning for the election of Bill Clinton to the Presidency, picking up a fairly Atlanticist attitude in my global outlook. All of these characteristics remained important to me, even though they fell far out-of-favour in the Labour Party more recently.

Having run out of money in that third year of my degree, I returned to Leeds University but lived back at home in Bingley, getting involved in the mainstream Labour Party rather than student politics. This meant that I had a shot at standing as a local councillor in a sea of Conservative seats in commuter-belt Bradford District, and in 1994 won a shock election as the first Labour councillor for Bingley in decades. Becoming involved in local government politics gave me an amazing grounding at an early age, I was able to work for an MEP part-time, take on a master's degree and broaden my studies into industrial and labour economics, and when the chance came to be selected for the parliamentary seat, I grabbed it. Against some local competition, I was selected to run for Labour against the Chairman of the Tory 1922 Committee, Sir Marcus Fox. Shipley had been Conservative for 45 years... but my timing was fortunate, and I found myself as the youngest MP in the Commons after 1 May 1997.

In the sweep of the great 1997 general election, I entered the Commons as MP for Shipley just as Tony Blair entered Number 10 as Prime Minister. It was a great time and we actually got to do some massive reforms benefitting millions of people. I held that seat in 2001 but lost by a whisker in 2005.

Representing a marginal seat sears into your outlook that the public matter first and foremost; that to make real change you need to convince the wider community, not just play to the gallery of local Labour Party activists.

After leaving Parliament in 2005, I then spent five years running a local government think tank campaigning on devolution and localism, also helping Gordon Brown as he took over the Labour leadership. I had been a minister in three different departments. I was the Minister for the Courts at Constitutional Affairs, oversaw local government in Prescott's department, and before that the Cabinet Office as well, and so I had a few strings to my bow. In 2010 I had the opportunity to go for the vacancy in Nottingham East at the retirement of John Heppell and was subsequently elected as Nottingham East MP on three occasions. And I was very lucky indeed, I had 18 years in the Commons, I had time in government, a lot of my colleagues never had that. But government was far more fulfilling and meaningful than Opposition. And it is something that sadly too many Labour MPs lost sight of in recent years.

Joan Ryan, MP for Enfield North, 1997–2010, and 2015–2019

Joan Ryan supporting the Royal British Legion

My mum and dad both came from Ireland. Their working lives were hard. They had manual jobs and often faced discrimination, but they wanted – and achieved – something better for their children. Good schools and my parents' hard work gave my sisters and I a great start in life, a university education and decent jobs. I learned from my mum and dad the dignity of work and the evil of racism and prejudice. I also saw, through the Irish Club my dad was part of, how people stuck together, helped each other through the hard times, and treated each other with fairness and decency; that experience led me to join the Labour Party. My politics and values were also shaped by the many years I spent in the classroom as a teacher before I became an MP.

I started work as a secondary school teacher in 1984 and I loved teaching, and I knew and still know that teaching is one of the most important, useful jobs anyone can undertake and if you want to make a difference then teaching is a wonderful way to do it. There is enormous satisfaction from helping young people fulfil their potential, find their ambition and aspire to more than they thought possible. Teaching more than anything made me determined to make a difference and not just for my own children but on a wider scale to do all I could give real opportunity to all young people. Such a determination leads to politics and standing for office. To be a part of where the decisions get made.

Prior to 1997, I was a councillor, serving as Deputy Leader of Barnet Council and was the Chair of Policy and Finance. My areas of key interest are education, health – including air pollution, and home affairs and foreign affairs – including conflict resolution and strengthening political institutions and democracy.

In the 1980s, I worked for a time as an oral historian at the Imperial War Museum, helping to capture the stories of civilians in the Second World War. I had the privilege to talk with many Holocaust survivors. I listened to people – children and teenagers at the time – tell the horrific stories of their time in work camps and ghettos, on forced marches, and at Auschwitz, Belsen, and Dachau. The memory of their experiences has stayed with me always. It is why I, and many others, share the determination of our Jewish fellow countrymen and women to never again allow anti-Semitism to enter the political mainstream. It is truly shaming that the Labour Party appeared so dismissive and nonchalant about their fears. The party would never have treated the anxieties of any other minority group in this way. I was horrified that so many people appeared willing to put this fundamental issue to one side because they viewed other issues as somehow more important. A vote for Corbyn would not only be a betrayal of the Jewish community, it would also be a betrayal of the values of equality and anti-racism that Labour once held dear. Anti-Semitism is not only an evil: it is corrosive to democracy and society. It is the ideology of cranks and conspiracy theorists, the calling-card of those who deal in fear and blame, rather than hope and generosity. All Britons, Jewish or not, should fiercely resist this kind of politics infecting our country's body politic.

I was a Member of the Committee of Selection, between November 2001 and May 2006.

I was a member of the Labour government, serving as an Assistant and Senior Government Whip from 2002 to 2006. In May 2006, I was appointed a minister in the Home Office, with responsibility for Citizenship, Immigration, Refugees, Police Forensics, Extradition and the Passport Service. From June 2007 to September 2008, I was the Prime Minister's Special Representative to Cyprus. I also served as the Vice-Chair of the Labour Party.

I was appointed to Privy Council 2007.

I feel enormously privileged to have served as a Member of Parliament and even more so to have served as a minister in the Labour government led by Tony Blair. I am proud of all that Labour achieved during the 1997 to 2010 period. I think we really did make a difference to life and opportunities for all in the UK and most especially in education opportunity, bringing real change and uplifting state education provision.

During my time away from Westminster from 2010 to 2015, I was the Chief Executive of the Global Tamil Forum, working on human rights and humanitarian issues in Sri Lanka. I was also the Chair of Riders for Health, from 2011–2015, a charity which has helped to improve access to life-saving

treatment and medical care for 21 million people across seven countries in sub-Saharan Africa. In addition, I worked as a training consultant strengthening democracy and parliamentary procedures as well as supporting Members of Parliament in Georgia, Uganda and women MPs from Iraq. I participated in the UNDP & IPU Induction Programme to train new MPs in the Myanmar Hluttaw (Parliament) in February 2016. I was the deputy director of the successful NO to AV national referendum campaign on the UK voting system.

I served as chair of Labour Friends of Israel from 2015–2019. In Parliament, I led the campaign to prevent UK aid being used by the Palestinian Authority to incite violence and glorify terrorism. I also worked with the Alliance for Middle East Peace to promote the establishment of an International Fund for Israeli-Palestinian Peace. Thanks to my efforts and others, the British government last year became the first in the world to endorse the Fund. Following my appointment by the Speaker of the House of Commons, I joined the Panel of Chairs in 2017. I was a member of the Environmental Audit Select Committee from December 2016. Its members chair Public Bill Committees and other general committees, as well as debates in Westminster Hall.

I was re-elected in the 2017 general election with an increased majority of 10,247.

In February 2019, I resigned from Labour over the failure of its hard-left leader, Jeremy Corbyn, to tackle anti-Semitism in the party. My resignation, which attracted widespread media coverage, sharply criticised Corbyn for "presiding over a culture of anti-Semitism and hatred of Israel". In autumn 2019, I announced that I would not be re-standing for Parliament.

Mike Gapes, MP for Ilford South, 1992–2019

Mike Gapes MP chairing the Political Committee of the NATO Parliamentary Assembly, Tirana Albania, May 2016.

I was always very interested in other countries. I collected stamps from an early age. My favourite subjects at school were geography and history. I think that played an important part in my political development. I got my politics from my dad, Frank, I think. He wasn't a member of any Party, but he was an active Trade Unionist in the Union of Post Office Workers, and he always voted Labour and read the *Daily Mirror*. He was a quiet, thoughtful man. But he talked to me about politics from an early age, patiently answering all my questions. And I think I got my ability to talk at length from my mum, Cis (Emily). My early years were spent in Woodford Bridge and Debden in Essex. When I was seven, we moved to a newly built council house in Grange Hill, Chigwell, on the edge of the huge Hainault Estate. I have fond memories of climbing the big Oak tree at the bottom of our garden. In 1964, I was one of a handful at Manford Primary school to pass the eleven plus. I was very left-wing as a teenager, and when I was 16, I joined the Wanstead and Woodford Labour

Party Young Socialists. The LPYS was controlled by the
secretive Trotskyist, Revolutionary Socialist League, through
its front organisation, the Militant Tendency, and its
newspaper 'Militant'. But our branch was one of the few non-
Militant branches in East London. And I never joined Militant.
As a sixth former at Buckhurst Hill County High School,
I decided to do a gap year after my 'A' levels before university.
I spent a year doing Voluntary Service Overseas, teaching
classes of 57 and 48 at a rural mission school in Swaziland, a
small, poor recently independent landlocked country next to
Apartheid South Africa and Portuguese colonial Mozambique.

Some students had interrupted education and were older than
me. That year abroad had a profound influence on me and my
attitude to politics, poverty, racism, and foreign policy and
development. I travelled a lot in the region in the holidays and
before I returned home in September 1972 to take up the
Marmaduke Levitt scholarship at Fitzwilliam College,
Cambridge to study Economics. I was immediately very active
in student politics. I joined all the left-wing, third world and
anti-racist political societies. I was on the Fitzwilliam College
Junior Combination Room (JCR) committee, and in March
1973 I was elected on the Left slate onto the Executive of the
Cambridge Students Union, CSU. Then in November 1973,
I was elected as the Non-Sabbatical Secretary of Cambridge
Students Union. I was also actively involved in the National
Organisation of Labour Students (NOLS). At the January
1974 NOLS Conference at the Owen's Park Hall of Residence
in Manchester, there was a walk out by half of the delegates.
I was then elected as the founder Convenor of the "Clause
Four" Group. We were left-wing democratic socialists, but we
were not Trotskyists. I was also a leading figure in the Broad
Left, an alliance of Labour, Communist, and non-aligned
Independent Socialists who were the largest group in the
National Union of Students. The main opposition in student
politics at that time was between the Broad Left and the

far-left International Marxist Group (IMG) and International Socialists (IS). After I finished my degree at Cambridge, in 1975, I went to Middlesex Polytechnic at Enfield for a year to do a Diploma in Industrial Relations and Trade Union Studies. This enabled me to stand for a third time to be Chair of the National Organisation of Labour Students. It was a case of third time lucky, I was elected in December 75, to take over in the summer of 76, as the non-sabbatical Chair of NOLS. Then six months after putting forward the proposal to the Party NEC, I was appointed as the first National Student Organiser of the Labour Party in June 1977.

I got actively involved with European youth politics. In May 1977, I became Vice President of CENYC, the Council of European National Youth Committees. I was also Chair of the International Committee of the British Youth Council when Peter Mandelson was the BYC Chair. I learnt a lot about politics internationally in the BYC and CENYC. I represented CENYC on the Presidium of the World Youth Festival in Havana, Cuba in August 1978, where – much to the annoyance of the Soviets and Cubans – I almost single-handedly held up and toned down the final Festival Declaration. I did the Student Organiser job for three years, then in June 1980, I was appointed to a research job in the International Department at Walworth Road.

In late 1982, I got selected as Prospective Parliamentary candidate for Ilford North, the constituency where I'd grown up and where my parents still lived. I was living in Putney at the time. 1983 was a terrible year to be a Labour candidate. Fighting on our manifesto policies of unilateral nuclear disarmament and leaving the European Economic Community without a referendum, I lost badly.

My political positions after my defeat in Ilford North in 1983, began to evolve. I had recognised that Labour had a real problem. No compromise with the electorate was not a winning strategy. We would not win power again unless we moved away from the Bennite policy positions of 1983. In contrast, Jeremy Corbyn has made clear in numerous speeches and articles over the years since 1983 that he remained committed to the policies on which he was first elected as MP for Islington North, and on which Labour was resoundingly defeated in 1983. Indeed, he would go much further. Labour has always, even in our brief unilateralist period, been pro-NATO, but Jeremy Corbyn consistently adopted anti-American policies and opposed NATO membership.

After our defeat, Michael Foot stood down, and Neil Kinnock was overwhelmingly elected by all three sections of the newly established Electoral College and became Labour leader. Neil and his Leader's office set out to modernise the Party, and shift power from the dysfunctional Head Office and the NEC towards the team around the Party Leader. I knew several of them, including Neil's Chief of Staff, Charles Clarke, very well. They regarded me as one of the handful of people in the Party Head Office that they could totally trust. Although I was not a head of department, I was called over to advise on major speeches and debates, and sometimes helped before Prime Ministers Questions. I was in the trenches with Neil, fighting the Trots, and working to make Labour re-electable long before Tony Blair benefitted from what Neil Kinnock (and John Smith) had achieved in the previous years. I was very disappointed when Neil wasn't elected as Prime Minister. So, years later, when I was asked "Are you a Blairite or a Brownite?" I would say, "No, I'm a Kinnockite." I was always a Kinnockite.

I had joined the International Department in 1980 as a research assistant to work on defence and disarmament and East-West relations and related international policy. I played a key role in writing the policy document "Defence and Security for Britain" published in 1984, and our subsequent statements and materials. Following the 1987 election, there was a reorganisation, and the International Department and the Research Department were merged to become the Policy Directorate, but with two Heads of Section beneath it. I was promoted to be the Head of the International Section of the Party. From 1988 until 1992 I was privileged to be at the centre of the debate on Labour's approach to foreign, defence and disarmament policy at the time of great change internationally in the Soviet Union and Central and Eastern Europe, and when under Neil Kinnock Labour dramatically ended the policy of unilateral nuclear disarmament. I was pleased to be a part of this historic process and was privileged to be a fly on the wall in many of those really important meetings.

In February 1990, I was selected to be candidate for Ilford South, the neighbouring constituency to where I had grown up. Ilford South was a seat we had to win if Neil Kinnock was to become Prime Minister. We had one of the five best results in the country. I got a 5.9% swing, and after a recount won by a 402-vote majority. I went into Parliament in May 1992 feeling very mixed emotions. I was personally elated but shattered by Labour not winning overall, and Neil Kinnock not being Prime Minister. Before he left as leader, Neil Kinnock put me straight away onto the Foreign Affairs Select Committee.

The death of his successor John Smith in 1994 came as a terrible shock. At the time, I would have been more inclined to support Gordon Brown than Tony Blair, but Brown didn't stand, and Blair clearly had something special about him. I had first met Tony Blair in 1982 when I had briefed him on Defence Policy, he was the Labour candidate in the Beaconsfield by-election. I was impressed by him. He asked all the right questions and was a good listener. I knew his partner Cherie from when we had both served on the Labour Co-ordinating Committee Executive a few years earlier. I became a very strong, if critical, supporter of Tony Blair. I didn't agree with everything he did. Some of his positioning made me feel uncomfortable. I was not at that time certain that we needed to change the totemic Clause Four, but in retrospect it was a vital symbolic moment. On most issues, Blair's instincts were right and, to use his own phrase, he got 'the big picture'. Don't get buried in the weeds, think of the big picture. I am sure John Smith would also have won in 1997. But Tony Blair gave us an additional reach beyond the Labour tribe and a landslide victory.

A few weeks after the election, I was asked to go into the Northern Ireland office as a Parliamentary Private Secretary in Mo Mowlam's team, working for Paul Murphy and Adam Ingram. Paul was the Political Development Minister; Adam was the Security Minister. This was an unpaid role, on the payroll vote, but not on the payroll. I had some knowledge of Northern Ireland from my NOLS and NUS Broad Left days when Clause Four had supported the non-sectarian and trade union backed "Better Life for All Campaign". I also had good friends in the moderate nationalist SDLP, and in the Irish Labour Party from my International Officer, Socialist International days. I strongly opposed the "Troops Out Movement", which was run by prominent far-left supporters of the Provisional IRA and endorsed by some left Labour MPs including Jeremy Corbyn and John McDonnell. I loved my two years in the Northern Ireland Office Team. They treated me like an extra minister. Due to the heavy demands on him, I often had to substitute for Paul Murphy at short notice. Before and during the negotiations, my job was to be the contact point in Parliament with MPs of all parties, for the Ministerial team who were often in Belfast. I also had to keep contact with the smaller Northern Ireland Parties, and community groups. I was in Belfast for the two weeks leading up to the Agreement. We could never have got that Agreement without the strong cooperation between the British and Irish governments, and the support of Bill Clinton, and George

Mitchell, his negotiator. The European Union also contributed a great deal of political support and most importantly put loads of money into the ex-prisoners' organisations and the development funds that went into some of the poorer communities, particularly in Belfast.

I had been outspoken in Parliament against anti-Semitism. In 1996 I had introduced a Private Members Bill to make Holocaust denial a criminal offence. I was a prominent member of Labour Friends of Israel and had been strongly critical of the Iranian regime. I had also supported the anti-terrorist legislation introduced by Labour. I had always supported the two states position in the Middle East and argued for a viable Palestinian State. When I was Chair of NOLS we had produced a leaflet which said, "Palestinians Have Rights Too". But I didn't believe that Jews should be driven into the sea and the State of Israel should be wiped off the face of the earth. That for my Islamist critics meant I was a "Zionist Islamophobe". In 2001 they delivered a glossy leaflet throughout the constituency saying, "Mike Gapes. No friend of the Muslims. A true friend of Israel. He represents Tel Aviv South, not Ilford South." Despite their support, the Conservative candidate Suresh Kumar failed miserably, and I maintained my 14,000 majority.

After the 2001 election, I was asked to be a PPS again, this time to Lord Jeff Rooker, the Immigration Minister in David Blunkett's team in the Home Office. David Blunkett is a phenomenal politician; I knew him well from my Labour Head office days. I enjoyed my year in the Home Office, although not as much as my time in Northern Ireland. In 2002, Jeff Rooker was moved in a reshuffle. I really didn't want to be the PPS in the Commons tearoom hearing everybody's local planning complaints. I no longer expected to be a minister, and decided I wanted to get back to my interests in Foreign Affairs and Defence. I was asked to be the Chair of the Westminster Foundation for Democracy, which I did for three very busy years from 2002-2005.

In late 2003, I got back onto the Defence Select Committee, which I had previously served on from 1999 to 2001. I was there until 2005. We visited Basra in Iraq in both May and December 2004, soon after the controversial 2003 intervention to remove the Baathist Fascist regime of Saddam Hussein.

In February and March 2003, my wife was seriously ill. I had been given time off by the whips because of this and the need to care for our three young children. I had an excuse to stay away from a difficult vote. But if I had abstained, people in the constituency and elsewhere would have assumed I was a rebel against Tony Blair. That would have been easier politically, but it was dishonest. It would also have been a betrayal of Iraqi Kurdish, socialist and democratic friends who I had known for many years. Joan Ryan was my whip at that time. I telephoned her to say I was coming in for the crucial vote. As a result of my vote for the Labour government motion in March 2003, I faced a lot of hostility locally. Thousands of my constituents were Muslims, and most of them had probably voted for me in 2001. I knew many were very angry with the position I took. My friend Barham Salih (later President of Iraq), of the Patriotic Union of Kurdistan, had come into Parliament to speak to Labour MPs. He thanked me for my support and gave an interview to the *Ilford Recorder* explaining why he, as an Iraqi Kurd and Sunni Muslim wanted an intervention to remove Saddam. Far-left groups, and local Ilford Islamists, saw my vote to intervene in Iraq as an opportunity to get rid of me. About 40 protestors, mainly from outside Ilford, disrupted my constituency advice surgery. I faced strong criticism at a hostile Labour General Committee, and a march and petition against me. But I just stood strong and firm and didn't back off. After a year or so, I began to again receive invitations to attend events from local Muslim organisations. In 2005, the Lib Dems campaigned against me entirely about Iraq. But although my majority was reduced from 14,000, I got re-elected with a majority of over 9,000.

After the election, I had initially intended to go back on the Defence Select Committee, but after Bruce George stood down, the chair was allocated to the Conservatives. I decided to return to the Foreign Affairs Committee. I was put forward by the Labour Party to be the chair. As I said at the time, the next best thing to being Foreign Secretary is to be Chair of the Foreign Affairs Select Committee under a Labour government. Highlights of my five years included questioning a living God, the Dalai Lama. His evidence session was a media fest, with members of the public queuing to get in and several overflow rooms. Before we began, he foraged in a bag and pulled out something and said, "Ah, sweetie." He is a really clever media performer. Afterwards, I had the visit from the Chinese Ambassador, Fu Ying, who went on to become Foreign Minister in China. She came with a démarche, a letter of complaint, from the National People's Congress and a series of books about the CIA's role in Tibet.

We also visited China as part of the inquiry, where our committee was told there would be "serious consequences" if we went ahead with our decision to also go to Taiwan. As we see China continue to rise in global influence, the UK government, British companies, and our parliamentarians are likely to get more of that bullying in the future. The only way to deal with a bully is to stand resolute and stick to your principles.

Our committee did an ongoing inquiry into "Foreign Policy Aspects of the War on Terror". Foreign Secretary Jack Straw was furious with me when we criticised the government for assisting the US rendition of prisoners. He called me to angrily insist it was not true. Three years later, successor Foreign Secretary, David Miliband, had to make a special statement apologising to Parliament that the government had misled it about rendition by the US via the British Indian Ocean Territory, Diego Garcia, of two prisoners to Guantanamo Bay, Cuba, which had occurred when Jack Straw was Foreign Secretary. In 2006, I led a delegation from the FAC to Guantanamo Bay. Later that year, we went to Belmarsh Prison for a comparison to see the maximum-security prison for terrorists in this country. The detailed report of our visit recommended that Guantanamo could not simply be shut. Some of the people there were extremely dangerous. The US should transfer some prisoners to the US mainland, and the UK and the international community should assist in taking others.

The role of a Select Committee Chair is quite complicated because you are not there to speak for the government, but to scrutinise them. I was given a big media profile because of my role. Government Ministers often want to avoid the media on sensitive or difficult matters. I often received invitations to be the Labour voice, but I always tried very hard to make sure it was as a critical friend, I made clear I was not there to speak for the government, but as an informed voice who happened to be a Labour MP. Those five years, from 2005 to 10, were my best in Parliament. It was intensive, hard work, but I loved it. I had a very high profile as Chair of the Select Committee, loads of media, loads of speaking at meetings, loads of international visitors, and far too much travel. If we'd have had a Labour government in 2010, I would have been able to stay for a second term, but I knew that it would not be possible if we lost. The FAC, like the Treasury Committee, has always been chaired by a member of the governing party.

I decided, however, that my experience might be useful and was re-elected by the Parliamentary Party to stay on as an ordinary member of the Committee, in opposition under Richard Ottaway, 2010–15, Crispin Blunt, 2015–17 and then Tom Tugendhat, from 2017. Then Ian Austin and I were vindictively purged by the whipped vote of Corbyn Labour in April 2019, after we had resigned from the Party. It is worth noting that Labour never purged the people who joined the SDP in the 80s, they let them stay on the Select Committees. That's what they mean by the kinder, gentler politics, I presume.

CHAPTER TWO

The Labour Leadership Contest
and Its Aftermath

"If Corbyn gets elected, it's going to be a disaster, for the Party, for the country"

The starting point for any story is debatable, but all five of our authors agree that the 2015 general election was key and so as good a place as any to begin.

The 2015 General Election

Chris Leslie: It's important to start with the context of how things got to where they did, and in 2020, it's a five-year story. The 2015 general election was the last time I really felt that I wanted my team to succeed, thrive, and do well, because it chimed with my general outlook on the world. I wasn't particularly wild about Ed Miliband per se. He had a slightly wishy-washy position on the soft left, but it was generally a progressive, noble cause underpinned by a belief in a well-regulated market economy; a society that was more equal, but also looking after the most vulnerable, and understanding that we were in a global society in the modern era.

Mike Gapes: I had backed David Miliband in 2010 and was not surprised when his brother Ed took us to defeat in 2015. This was largely due to his misguided "year zero" strategy of disowning our past and failing to defend the record of the Blair and Brown governments.

Chris Leslie: I ended up with a very important role in the run up to the 2015 election; I was Shadow Chief Secretary to the Treasury in that Shadow Cabinet. I'd spent all my waking hours campaigning; advocating for Labour on the media, leading for Labour in the televised economy debates, including BBC Daily Politics with Andrew Neil, on a regular basis. Looking back, I remember one tough interview in particular, it was the anniversary of the "Ed Stone", Ed Miliband's carving in stone of the pledges. I was the poor soul wheeled out the Sunday before that general election finding myself having to defend this initiative, which I had nothing to do with. Andrew Neil asked me, *"Do you have planning permission for Number 10 Downing Street to put this in the back garden?"* I had to wing it, not easy! I put my back into the whole thing and, of course, after the 2015 general election defeat, Miliband went very quickly and there was a void.

The Labour Leadership Campaign

Mike Gapes: Labour was now in a very dangerous place, requiring an honest assessment of the reasons why we had lost in both 2010 and 2015. I was one of the people who backed the brave *"eat your greens"* candidate, Liz Kendall. But the membership was not interested in that difficult message. They also rejected the submarine strategy of experienced former minister Yvette Cooper, and the flip-flop, Andy Burnham.

Chris Leslie: Certain of my colleagues emerged into that leadership campaign: Burnham, Cooper, Liz Kendall, and, of course, Corbyn was in that race as well. Simultaneously, on the other side of politics, Cameron and Osborne were moving ahead. They'd won the election, and they were moving on.

It was clear that Labour had lost for a number of reasons. It had looked too cosy between Miliband and the SNP, and as though they were going to break up the United Kingdom, and that did not go down very well at all. Miliband also laid down those early signs that we were somehow becoming "anti-business". He was castigating any sort of private sector activity and moralising about behaviours. I think you can do that up to a point, and there are, of course, cretinous, exploitative activities in the private sector, but I think he alienated too many ordinary people by sounding anti-private sector.

Mike Gapes: At that time, in 2015, most of the pre-existing membership did not want to be challenged, they wanted a comfort blanket. Tens of thousands of new members joined or re-joined to support the far-left outsider Jeremy Corbyn. Under Ed Miliband's £3 membership scheme, many came in from the Greens, and various far-left groups, ex-Trots who'd been expelled from the party or left it in the 1970s, 1980s, and 1990s. There were also some enthusiastic young people, inspired by, and giving support to, an elderly white man, who had never held a position of responsibility in his 32 years in Parliament. This was a similar phenomenon, I suppose, to the support base of Bernie Sanders in the USA Democratic primaries a year later.

Chris Leslie: I felt that the lesson we needed to take forward after the 2015 election was to try and broaden out and look at society, to have a story to tell at a wider level. When Harriet Harman took over as the interim Labour leader, I was asked to step up as Shadow Chancellor for a few months. My general feeling was, *"Look, we have to do some really difficult things to show in these early days after the defeat that we are capable of learning lessons about why we've been beaten, confronting our weaknesses, and making us look fitter for the next time"*. Beginning the task of 'heavy lifting' was my focus. But while I was stretching the elastic in that direction, starting to confront the tough decisions a party needs to take to get itself back into contention with the wider public, the membership of the Labour Party was going in quite the opposite direction, into a sort of comfort zone, almost a foetal position, and regressing to the instincts of purity and ideology. Having been defeated, they were yearning for days gone by, as in the 1970s: *"Well, the world hates us, and we don't care."* From this situation, the kernel of Corbynism germinated, and, as bad luck would have it, the circumstances of the time, and especially

PETER McNAB

Labour's constitution, made it quite an open path for Corbyn to travel.

The Labour Party's change to the leadership rules and how it affected the race

Ann Coffey: Although Ed Miliband was criticised for changing the rules on leadership elections, he has always pointed out that the MPs failed in their gatekeeper role; Jeremy Corbyn got the necessary number of MPs supporting him to be nominated as a candidate. A number of those MPs shared my views about his unfitness to be leader, but they wanted "to *widen the debate*".

Chris Leslie: I was always very uncomfortable with the rule changes that were put in place by Ed Miliband; it put the entire future of the party in the hands of the party membership rather than the electoral college, between MPs, who at least provided some semblance of a voice for the general public in there. As it was all about the membership, MPs were quite emasculated during the leadership process, and so an internal party populism took hold, and this section was only concerned with which candidate was the "purist". Ironically, this was also happening in the Conservative Party. There was a mirror image process going on with regard to Brexit and their membership. What tends to happen in these circumstances is that the candidate who plays mostly to that base, thrives, and anybody who comes along and sounds as though they're telling the base, *"Actually, it's not all about your views, it's*

36

about the country," will fail; that was quite visible, and in both parties.

As it became clearer that Corbyn might win, it became clearer to our authors that they must speak out about the consequences

Chris Leslie: All of this culminated in the summer of 2015 where Corbyn was able to play all the old tunes including, *"We don't want the Blairites and their Iraq War,"* and the whole business about tearing down capitalism and all of its failings.

As Shadow Chancellor at the time, I felt it my duty to warn the membership that Corbyn was a bad idea. I remember speaking to my local constituency party, saying, *"If Corbyn gets elected, it's going to be a disaster for the party, for the country."* There were a lot of newer members, including retired teachers and college lecturers who wanted what they called a *"radical break"* from the Blair/Brown years. My entreaties fell on deaf ears; I was pleading with them, *"Please have an eye to the electorate, and what is in the real world."* But they wanted what they perceived as purity, rather than electability.

Mike Gapes: Like most Labour MPs, I knew it was now going to be very difficult for our party if Corbyn won. But unlike most MPs, I did not remain quiet. I decided to speak out publicly. In an article entitled "What Would a Jeremy Corbyn Foreign Policy Mean for Labour?" for the "Left Foot Forward" blog on 13 August

2015, I wrote: *"If Jeremy becomes Labour leader next month his anti-nuclear, anti-NATO, anti-American, anti-interventionist and Eurosceptic message will be welcomed by some in this country and by some abroad. But it is unlikely to be welcomed by Kurdish and other anti-Da'esh forces in Iraq, by anti-Assad democrats in Syria, by democratic Central European NATO states like Poland, or by Ukrainians."*

Ann Coffey: I did not vote for Jeremy Corbyn in the 2015 Labour leadership election. I thought his narrow sectarian views and poor leadership skills would be disastrous for the Labour Party and the people who looked to the party to provide an alternative government to the Conservatives. I thought his views on several issues more suited to the challenges of early 20th century industrial Britain than a country facing the challenges of a global economy in a digital age. His understanding of fairness and equality reduced complex moral issues to an attempt to assemble opposing armies on a tribal battlefield. Like all leaders, he surrounded himself with people who agreed with him. I thought his own political history and support for organisations with extreme views and his apparent lack of enthusiasm for Queen and country would not be very acceptable to many people we relied on to support us at elections.

Mike Gapes: I had been writing a regular diary to my daughter Rebecca, who had died suddenly aged 19 in 2012, in which I conveyed my innermost thoughts. I found it helped me deal with the grieving process and my continuing sense of loss. While I was on holiday in Cornwall on 29 August 2015, I wrote these words to Rebecca: *"It looks like the new Messiah is going to win. I will not accept his policies, and I will not capitulate to the cult of J.C. But I'm not yet sure how to play it. Open, full-frontal rebellion will be more honest, but may be tactically wrong. But I have nothing personally to lose. I don't expect to be a candidate in 2020 now. I've almost reconciled myself to retiring then, when I will be 67. The boundary changes may abolish Ilford South, and if they don't, I expect moves to deselect me. I will make no decisions now but will review this at Christmas."*

Jeremy Corbyn was elected as leader of the Labour Party

Mike Gapes: 12 September 2015 was the day the leadership ballot result was announced. I put a tweet out at 9.30am which said, *"Yesterday, Parliament voted against assisted suicide. Today, the Labour Party brings it back for political parties."*

Ann Coffey: Jeremy Corbyn won the leadership election in all 3 sections in the first round with 59.5% of the votes.

Joan Ryan: Many people underestimated the profound transformation the election of Jeremy Corbyn as leader brought about.

Chris Leslie: I assumed, *"Well, that's the end of my time on the front bench. There's absolutely no compatibility between my views and those of Corbyn.*" I knew that was the beginning of quite a long period in the wilderness for me. It was quite symbolic of the time, going into my office on the Monday after Corbyn got elected and finding all my office possessions in black bin bags outside the door. John McDonnell and his team had arranged to tip all my desk contents into the corridor. That's a by-the-by, in a way, but it was also a totemic change of direction for the Labour Party – they literally regarded us and previous Labour administrations as history to be disposed of.

There were huge philosophical differences between the two parts of the Party

Chris Leslie: We were in the centre-left social democratic model of political philosophy, while Corbyn and his team were very much a kind of modern Marxist, and anti-capitalist group, and those views reached across a whole series of areas, including their attitudes to things like Trident renewal and, of course, on the European question, which was the big one running up to the 2016 European referendum. They regarded the EU as a sort of capitalist club. Corbyn had always been of that view. If you believe that in a modern global world you have to trade and do business across borders in a pragmatic way, you were pro-EU, and that was another pretty big cultural divide. Corbyn deliberately didn't really do anything in that referendum. When the result came out, he said, "Let's trigger Article 50," pretty much straightaway. Ann Coffey will tell you that a lot of us were really quite fed up at the time, and we wanted to move the Labour Party back into contention. It was clear to me that the European result was absolutely a moment of reckoning, a clear and defining example of how Corbyn's world view was actively harming our whole country's future and the first real attempt to do something about Corbyn and his leadership.

Ann Coffey: It was quite clear that, although Jeremy Corbyn had accepted the leadership of a pro-European party, he himself was far from being pro-EU. His voting record in Parliament provided ample evidence of that. He did little to support the Remain campaign. He would not share a platform with David Cameron. His antipathy to campaigning with "Tories" was, I think, partly to do with his view that politics should be tribal, and partly that he believed that the EU was an international capitalist conspiracy.

Chris Leslie: I felt very uncomfortable with the hard-left populist approach that would throw any ideas of responsibility and governing with a willingness to confront difficult choices to one side, in the hope of winning on the back of what I regarded as a fairly false prospectus. Offering to cure the world's ills with unlimited resources that could just be magicked up. For example, I was very resistant to Corbyn and McDonnell taking over the country with the financial risk that they posed, and, although the nation's finances today have taken a turn for the worse, I truly believe they would have had no regard at all to issues of affordability and destabilised Britain's fiscal reputation and created a crisis in the UK government's relations with the markets.

It was very disheartening and a lot of us who had been in the Shadow Cabinet at the time began to meet fairly regularly, "in exile". We stared at each other in disbelief and horror at what was happening. Straight after Corbyn's arrival as leader in September 2015, many of those who'd served in Ed Miliband's shadow cabinet chose to leave the frontbench. Many of us felt similarly and so – perhaps as a support group initially – we started to meet routinely on a Monday lunchtime in Tristram Hunt's office to regroup and figure out, *"Well, what are we going to do? How do we cope in these circumstances? How long is this period of the wilderness years going to go on for?"*

I had never imagined finding myself focusing on organising internally, when before I'd always been involved in policy making, and not in what you might call "organisational politics", particularly. It was really at that point that I started to co-ordinate a little bit more in the Parliamentary Labour Party, across the range of figures who knew the Corbyn-McDonnell project was nuts, and who needed to come together and do something about it, rather than simply wait for years and years while the country was left without a viable Opposition.

Mike Gapes: I decided I could not be silent. I had to speak out for the policies and values of sensible

Labour politics. I got "Tweet of the Day" in the Daily Mirror at the start of the Labour Conference for: *"Early start. First train from Ilford. Check map. 2015 Manifesto. 1983 Manifesto. Book on Trotskyist history. Tin hat."* I also got mentioned in the Guardian for: *"No raddled old SWP Trot is going to tell me or other Labour MPs how to vote."* I made media waves by saying publicly that there was no coherence and no credible economic policy. On 8 October I told Radio 5 Live that I would be as loyal to Corbyn as he had been to successive Labour leaders, Michael Foot, Neil Kinnock, John Smith, Tony Blair and Gordon Brown, when he had voted over 500 times against the Labour whip.

On 9 October while attending a NATO Parliamentary Assembly meeting at Stavanger, Norway, I wrote in my diary, *"I'm not happy with the government position on Syria, but it is preferable to the pro-Putin, pacifist hand wringing, coming from the Messiah and his acolytes."* I wrote, *"There is no Corbyn bounce. Cameron and Osborne have had a free hit against Labour as extremists with terrorist sympathisers as leader and Shadow Chancellor."* I went on, *"The far-left organisation 'Momentum' will be a front for pressurising and deselecting MPs. They have thrown down the gauntlet and I intend to fight back. I will campaign hard locally and represent my constituents and enjoy myself until the end, whenever it comes. I may go quietly but it is possible I will have to cause a big bang byelection in 2019 if Corbyn is still leader then and is taking us to defeat"*. Little did I know then how prescient those inner thoughts were to become.

It wasn't just those within the Labour Party who were unhappy with the situation though; there were also Conservative MPs who were becoming increasingly dissatisfied with the situation.

Anna Soubry: Let me give you a really good example of how that has screwed up British politics leading to this need to do things differently. The coalition government said, *"We are going to involve real people in planning decisions. You are going to have a much better say in your location about the future."* That sounds absolutely brilliant; isn't that an admirable principle? That's great. They said, *"And so, when planning applications are made, you can now directly get involved in the process by making your views known."* How can you not like that, that's brilliant, right? I get that, that's marvellous. So, I had the Planning Minister, the lovely Nick Boles, come to a meeting of one of my Town Councils, and they'd already told me about this. Kimberley Town Council say it as it is, no messing about. Nick said, *"But isn't this marvellous, you can now get involved in the planning decisions?"* They said, *"Really? Have you seen the form?"* He said, *"Sorry?"* They said, *"Have you seen the form?"* I'd had them print it off and they showed it to him. And he went, *"Oh, my God."* They said, *"Yeah."* He said, *"But this is – how can you make your...?"* *"Exactly."* *"You can't really make your views known."* *"No, that's right."* And he had no idea. He'd sat in a meeting when we introduced this legislation to involve people, but he'd never asked, *"Can I see the form? Can I actually see it and understand the process by which a real human being fills this in?"*

I always used to say this to people, *"Imagine it's somebody who owns the shop that you shop in, or your neighbour, or your mum, or your brother, or your sister, or whoever, a real human being. How would they access that form and then how do they make their views known?"* Not understanding how real people live their lives is one of the things that really hacks people off about politicians.

Politicians go on the media and they say, *"We've got a different way of doing it now – you can have your say."* And the viewer or listener sits there and says, *"That's crap,"* and they shout at the radio, *"that's crap,"* or throw things at the telly. *"It's not – it's crap, I've been on that website, I've seen that form, you can't fill it in, it doesn't allow you to do it. It's only there for developers, it's not there for ordinary citizens."* And that's when you get the breakdown in trust and that leads to populism because someone who actually doesn't give a monkey about real ordinary folk, comes along and says, *"You are left behind, they don't really care about you, they don't understand your lives."* They don't even know that you have to be a property developer to fill in that form, it's actually not for you, the little guy, it's for their rich mates, because they don't care about you.

When I was a minister, there were so many examples. During and after the floods, I'd go out on visits to affected areas and I'd say to people, *"So, have you got your money for flood relief?"* "No." So, I'd turn to my team and say, *"Hang on, why haven't got their money?"* The answer would be, *"Oh, well, it takes three weeks to process."* And I said, *"But we agreed it would not take weeks to process we agreed to make the money available immediately... so let's do it... now."*

CHAPTER THREE

The "Birthday Club" WhatsApp Group

"Don't forget, at that time most of us had never felt the need to 'rebel' as MPs"

Chris Leslie: I set up a series of WhatsApp groups. WhatsApp was a new thing at the time as a way for MPs to co-ordinate and network and keep in touch. I set up what became an infamous way of communicating across relatively moderate Labour MPs. We called it the "Birthday Club". We had to think of a random fairly innocuous name for it, just in case we were discovered. Don't forget, at that time most of us had never felt the need to "rebel" as MPs, let alone organise against the internal approach of the party leadership. It was actually the pretext of Tristram Hunt's birthday where we managed to go and have dinners together occasionally, off-site in Covent Garden and elsewhere, and try and get a wider group of like-minded MPs together. (Tristram left in January 2017 to become the Director of the Victoria & Albert Museum.) In fact, I ended up with about 86 Labour MPs at one point on that WhatsApp group; all sharing their exasperation and horror with the various things that were going on. It makes interesting reading!

Mike Gapes: My assumption was that Labour would have to, at some point, try to get a credible leadership and in a similar way to what had happened to George Lansbury in 1935. He led the Labour Party from 1932 until 1935. His Christian pacifist stance was initially very popular with Labour members but was opposed by the trade unions. At the 1935 Party conference, the national executive tabled a resolution calling for sanctions against Italy following the Mussolini invasion of Abyssinia. Lansbury spoke in opposition to this as a form of economic warfare. His speech was well received by the delegates, but immediately destroyed by Ernest Bevin, leader of the Transport and General Workers Union, who attacked Lansbury for putting his private beliefs before a policy agreed by all the party's main institutions to oppose fascist aggression and accused him of "hawking your conscience round from body to body asking to be told what to do with it". Union support ensured that the sanctions resolution was carried by a huge majority; Lansbury resigned a few days later.

I hoped that someone in the Trade Unions and the NEC, someone on the sane left, would go to Corbyn and say, *"You're not going to win, you're going to drag the party down"*. But it didn't happen. He clung on.

Meanwhile, important events were playing out in Parliament, and some of these were significant to our story. The build-up

to the Syria Vote in 2015, which was yet another issue that reflected values that weren't shared by all.

Chris Leslie: At one point, when Assad had been chemically attacking the towns and cities within Syria and children were dying; the joint security forces then identified that there was a cache of chemicals that Assad was about to use. The question that was increasingly raised was, "Shouldn't something be done to take that out?" I felt, of course it should! If that could be done with minimal civilian casualties, then, of course, you've got a duty to protect those people from chemical attacks by Assad. It was about saving lives, and I certainly felt that that responsibility weighed on me as an MP. I had to represent the whole community, not just the party membership, and I had to do what I felt was right. I don't believe in walking by on the other side. I think if you can do the responsible thing and help other people at risk of humanitarian distress, then you've got a duty to do it in the responsible way. This whole question of 'responsibility' in office is right at the heart of so many of the disagreements that we had. So along with other Labour MPs, we gave our support to the government in taking action, and deterring Assad, as it turned out only for a further year, but it definitely had an impact. And I called out Corbyn in the Commons statement with the Prime Minister, urging MPs not just to hold the government to account, but also those who through inaction were also choosing a course with its own terrible consequences as well. I am proud to have taken a stand at that crucial moment.

The Syria Vote, November 2015

Chris Leslie: In November 2015 there were the atrocities of the Islamic State in Syria, and Corbyn was refusing to countenance anything that would constrain them in Syria. There was a big vote in the Commons, and that was one of the early rebellions that we had to have; 66 Labour MPs voted that actions should be allowed in Syria to constrain ISIL. It was there, on the defence and national security side of things, that you started to see the early signs of major differences of opinion breaking out into the open. In the wake of that, Michael Dugher and Pat McFadden were sacked in the Shadow Cabinet reshuffle, and that also exacerbated the situation. From time-to-time, people would speak out; I spoke out in Parliament, at PLP meetings on a Monday night, and these meetings became increasingly heated. It became even more clear that there were different tribes and different values within the party.

Mike Gapes: My high-profile criticism of Corbyn meant I was under a lot of attack from abusive Trots and other trolls on Twitter. This contributed to a lot of stress at that time. My public criticism was not liked by a large number of members of my local party. A motion of censure calling on me to keep my critical views private was passed by one of my branches and then came to the General Committee in October. It narrowly passed at a very unpleasant meeting with a lot of aggression and shouting. But I robustly refused to be gagged. I was travelling a lot around that time, I was on the NATO

Parliamentary Assembly, and the Foreign Affairs Committee, and I had recently been made the Honorary President of Labour International, the organisation for Labour members in other countries.

In October and November 2015, the amount of travelling that I was doing was ridiculous. I went abroad seven times in nine weeks, including visiting Iraqi Kurdistan. The next week I was in Egypt, Jordan and Lebanon with the Foreign Affairs Select Committee.

Mike Gapes' Illness

Mike Gapes: We flew back from Beirut overnight on Thursday, arriving at Heathrow in the morning on 27 November. I wasn't feeling very well. I had some pains that I thought was indigestion but nevertheless went back into London on the tube from Ilford into central London that evening to join my friends at the Jools Holland concert at the Royal Albert Hall. I felt ill in the interval and didn't feel strong enough to go up and get a drink. At the end of the concert, I collapsed outside on the street.

They scanned me in Chelsea and Westminster Hospital and immediately phoned through to St Mary's Paddington, which is a top heart hospital, and I was rushed there. When we arrived at St Mary's, it was like a scene from *Casualty*, with about 10 people in high-vis jackets waiting for me. They rushed me down into the operating theatre, straight away, on the trolley, and the consultant said, "*Where have you been?"* I said, *"Well, I'm a Member of Parliament, I've been in Lebanon, and I've just got back."* He said, *"We have injected you with anaesthetic, which could take a little while to work, but I'm afraid I've got to start straight away."* I was in an induced coma for three weeks and in intensive care for six weeks.

I came out of hospital on the 20 January 2016, I then spent the next two months at home, slowly getting back my muscle strength. I went back to Parliament, too early probably, in late March. I did not feel able to walk fast or run for a bus until the autumn. That close encounter with death has shaped my thinking on everything I now do in politics and life. Every day is a bonus. When I came out of hospital, I vowed I wasn't going to prevaricate anymore. I was still frail, so I wasn't able to campaign as much as I wanted in the EU referendum or the London Mayoral campaign, because I was still getting my strength back, but I still did a fair bit.

CHAPTER FOUR

The EU Referendum Result and Its Aftermath, 2016

"This PLP has no confidence in Jeremy Corbyn as leader of the Parliamentary Labour Party"

In 2016 David Cameron called for a referendum on EU membership, and on June 23 the UK voted to leave the EU by 51.9 % to 48.1%. Shortly afterwards, Cameron resigned, and Theresa May was elected as Conservative leader and Prime Minister.

Mike Gapes: I was disgusted by Corbyn's pathetic role in the European campaign and his lukewarm "seven and a half out of ten" support. I was incredulous and furious when Corbyn said we should trigger Article 50 on the first day after the referendum defeat.

Chris Leslie: Straight after that referendum result, talking with my wife Nicola and thinking about what we needed to do to prevent Corbyn creating even greater chaos for the party and the country, a classic leadership challenge didn't quite feel as though it would get sufficient traction, although there were enough people in the Labour Party who were very fed up with Corbyn's performance in that European referendum and who were willing to voice that. We decided on a "vote of no confidence" in Corbyn's leadership in the Parliamentary Labour Party. Although that wasn't something that existed as a formal constitutional device, we knew that we had the right to bring motions before the PLP, just like any member could bring a motion before a CLP meeting, so we did. It allowed us to focus – in principle – on the dangers that Corbyn posed if allowed to continue.

Chris Leslie: Hilary Benn made his big speech as shadow foreign secretary opposing Corbyn's line on Syria and Assad in December 2015, but he continued as shadow foreign secretary until the weekend after the referendum result. The 'vote of no confidence' motion was tabled by Margaret Hodge and Ann Coffey, which prompted Hilary Benn to telephone several others in the shadow cabinet to discuss what they'd do. The Leader's office discovered this and issued a statement on 25th June saying they were sacking Hilary but, in reality, Hilary was resigning almost simultaneously. That flash point prompted Heidi Alexander and then many others to also follow him and resign from Corbyn's shadow Cabinet. The vote of no confidence in the PLP then proceeded after that weekend on 28th June.

No Confidence Motion, 28 June 2016

Ann Coffey: Margaret Hodge MP tabled a motion for debate: *"This PLP has no confidence in Jeremy Corbyn as leader of the Parliamentary Labour Party"*, and I seconded it.

Chris Leslie: Margaret and Ann were fearless. And the great thing about that device was it didn't mean colleagues had to support an alternative candidate to Corbyn. It was a free-standing motion that was hard for the majority to resist, morally, because in their hearts they knew truthfully that they had no confidence in Corbyn or in his philosophy. Following a secret ballot (a very important element in the process), the result was that 80% of Labour MPs voted that they had no confidence in him, and that triggered a series of resignations from the Shadow Cabinet, including Hilary Benn, and Heidi Alexander, and various others.

Ann Coffey: The vote was carried by 172 to 40. Jeremy Corbyn did not resign and there followed a challenge to his leadership of the Labour Party. The National Executive Committee ruled that he should automatically be included on the ballot paper without the requirement for 20% of MPs and MEPs to nominate him. Would those MPs who nominated him in 2015 "to widen the debate" have done so again? We'll never know, and the rest is history.

Chris Leslie: That tumbled into quite a crisis for Corbyn, which nearly prised him out of the leadership, but there were some, what you might call the 'old Right' position, the Tom Watson brigade, who didn't really feel as though they had control over what was going on, and so irritatingly they tried to slow this process down, and in doing so, there was a week or two's breathing space given to Corbyn while Watson engaged in the futile effort of trying to persuade Len McCluskey to move to another position.

The Process of Choosing a Candidate

Mike Gapes: When Corbyn insisted he would not resign, I backed Angela Eagle to challenge him, but a group of younger MPs did not want anyone who had been an MP from the Blair/Iraq era, and so Owen Smith was chosen to challenge Corbyn.

Chris Leslie: Tom Watson certainly didn't like the idea of Angela Eagle as a challenger, as he wanted Owen Smith. After much wrangling, Angela stood aside, and Tom Watson's view favouring Owen Smith as the challenger prevailed. By then, it was too late. Corbyn had been persuaded by, presumably John McDonnell and others, that he could simply ignore the motion of no confidence passed in the PLP as it had no formal standing. He could disregard them, knowing that he didn't have to care about it, and, of course, that's basically what he did. He didn't care about the vote of no confidence, and decided, well, "Sod you!" We had lost the element of surprise and allowed them to regroup. It all went back to the membership, and the membership still didn't want to move to a more pragmatic, more electable position under Owen Smith; they wanted to stay with that utopian view, and so Corbyn was re-elected. It was a very hard time indeed and tremendously dispiriting. We tried everything, a lot of devices, to shake the madness out of the Labour Party.

Mike Gapes: On the flight home from Shanghai where I had been with a NATO Parliamentary Assembly delegation, on 30 July 2016, I wrote in my diary, *"If (or when) Corbyn wins again there will be four consequences: 1. MPs like me will still have no confidence in him; 2. Theresa May may be tempted to call an early election in the autumn or spring; 3. Labour will be wiped out; and 4. Corbyn activists and clicktivists will move to deselect 'disloyal' MPs"*. I went on, *"I am uncertain what to do. But I am advised not to raise my blood pressure!... It may now be time to go..."*

Ann Coffey: Jeremy Corbyn won with an increased share of the vote. I understand why party members and supporters re-elected Jeremy Corbyn. Being part of a movement can be an enticing clarion call, but I did not think the wider public were engaged by the movement. I was extremely disappointed as I thought we would never win a general election with him as our leader. Some party members were very opposed to Tony Blair as leader and pointed out that they had accepted his leadership. However, the difference was that the general public liked and responded to Tony Blair as evidenced by the Labour Party's huge majority in 1997. It is no use having a leader who is only liked by his own party, however.

In the aftermath, some Labour MPs returned to the front bench; others joined the anti-Corbyn "Birthday Club" WhatsApp group. At the same time, rumblings in the Conservative Party continued, and there were some who found a growing affinity with members of the Labour Party.

Anna Soubry: As time went by, I would look at the people I was voting with, and I started to get to know people like Chris Leslie and Liz Kendall; in addition, they were East Midlands MPs like me, so, I was working with them on other local stuff. I'd look at them and think, "I've got more in common with this person than I have with that person, and I'm in the same political party as that other person." After the EU referendum, the Conservative Party changed and I became more vocal, which said a lot. I was *increasingly* in the same lobby as members of the Labour Party like Chris and Chuka, Wes Streeting, Pat McFadden, Mike Gapes, and many others. I remember saying, *"This is ridiculous, why aren't we in the same party? We have so much more in common,"* – that expression, that wonderful Jo Cox expression, *"More in common."* We have more in common and I certainly had more in common, I felt, with them, than I did, increasingly, with a significant swathe of Conservatives, who now, by 2016, had won. They'd not just won the referendum, but they'd also won that longstanding battle between the One Nation Tories that Ken represented and the reactionary right wing of the party that had driven me out of the Conservative Party back in the early 80s. These guys, and they tend to be guys, were in control and May was dancing to their tune.

The Impact of Theresa May's Speech in 2016 and Amber Rudd's on Immigration

Anna Soubry: In 2016, there were two things that really, really struck a chord of profound concern in me. The first was May's speech when she talked about this Liberal metropolitan elite; that was, basically, my mother, and people like my mother, who voted Remain. My mother is from North Nottinghamshire. She has never moved more than 15 miles from the place where she was born, in Worksop. She's not metropolitan by any stretch of the imagination and to describe her as a Liberal is probably one of the greatest insults you could give her. She met my father when they were both in the Young Conservatives, but they were McMillanite One Nation Tories. Is she a member of the elite? I mean, for God's sakes, she was a radiographer at Doncaster Royal Infirmary. It was just like, "How more insulting could you be to people?" May also said in a speech to the Conservative Party conference, "If you're a citizen of the world, you're a citizen of nowhere." I was appalled and thought, "Dear God, this woman is our Prime Minister," and this marked, to me, huge change in the Conservative Party.

The second thing was Amber Rudd's speech on immigration that sickened me to the bottom of my stomach, because I have always been a firm believer in the positive benefits of immigration over the centuries; to hear our Home Secretary, especially Amber of all people, just spouting this deeply concerning and insulting twaddle. This was a watershed to me, and the question became when I would leave; how could I stay, how could I? When I asked myself how all of this was going to work out, I knew that they had won, 'cause they'd won.

CHAPTER FIVE

Article 50 and the General Election, June 2017

"Where are we going with all this?"

On 29 March 2017 Theresa May triggered Article 50 that started the two-year timetable for the UK to withdraw from the EU. Despite saying that she wouldn't, on 18 April, May called a snap general election for 8 June.

Mike Gapes: Parliament was dominated by the internal Tory debate on Brexit, and Theresa May decided to trigger Article 50 in March 2017, even though the government had no agreed negotiating position. She then, as I had predicted, called an early general election. May did so at a time that the Tories were over 20 points ahead of Labour. She expected a big Conservative majority. So, did I. What neither of us had bargained for was the ineptitude and incompetence of the Tory campaign.

I decided I had to fight the early election. I expected my majority to fall from the 19,777 I had had in 2015 to around 10,000 and for my neighbour Wes Streeting, who had won in 2015 by only 589 votes, to lose. I sent all my activists into Ilford North to work for Wes and also campaigned there myself. I was delighted when

Wes Streeting's majority went up to almost 10,000. Despite doing almost no door knocking, I had my best ever result. A combination of a much higher turnout and my strong pro-European message saw my vote go up to over 43,000 and my majority increase to 31,647 as we won 75.8% of the vote. I had fought a campaign which did not mention Corbyn at all. The only Labour figure I used was London Mayor Sadiq Khan. On 16 June 2017, I wrote in my diary, *"I was completely wrong about the result. I'm now under pressure from Corbynistas to eat humble pie. But I won't. The fundamentals of his ideology and the sectarian Stalinist/Trot alliance behind him have not changed. I can't accept his pro-Putin/pro-Iran, quasi pacifist, ultra-left foreign policy."*

Ann Coffey: When I stood in 2015, I had decided that it would be my last term. In 2020 I would be 73, I would have spent 28 years as the MP for Stockport. The 2017 election was a surprise, and I think I stood as a reaction because I had not done the preparation for retirement. The election was an extremely uncomfortable experience. When I knocked on doors, I said, *"Well, you know, I don't support Jeremy Corbyn, but I do support the Labour Party."* The fact that I thought he would not be elected did not help to square the ludicrous position I had put myself in of campaigning to be elected as an MP for a party whose leader I thought was unfit to be Prime Minister. Obviously, that was untenable.

Chris Leslie: Theresa May decided Labour was in such a mess that she would go for an early general election. This exposed what a pretty atrocious campaigner she was herself, and she really couldn't cope with the scrutiny of a general election. Corbyn was very good at positioning himself as the underdog, held the tub-thumping public rallies, but when it didn't look as though there was any real threat of him actually getting elected, the public didn't need to take him seriously, and he managed to make it a fairly mild loss for Labour. It was still a loss, and that was the irony! Bizarrely, team Corbyn started framing yet another election loss as some sort of 'victory', which it certainly wasn't! I went on the Radio4 *Today Programme* a couple of days after and said, "Isn't it bad we've lost the general election?" and got more abuse than anybody else in the election on Twitter for daring to say we had actually lost! Incidentally, according to a Southampton University study that came out at the time, I got far more Twitter abuse for speaking that particular truth than anyone else in the party, more than Diane Abbott or others. As the election loss wasn't perceived as fatal for Labour, Corbyn continued.

Ann Coffey: Jeremy Corbyn's supporters falsely claimed that he had won the election because of a net gain of 30 seats. However, we had lost support in what came to be called the "Red Wall" seats. Canvassing in Stockport, I was more likely to get a warm reception from voters in four-bedroomed detached house than in areas that had provided our traditional support.

As the result was hailed as a triumph by his supporters, Momentum gained in strength. The sectarianism and increasing unpleasantness as a result of Momentum's growing activity in the party was all too reminiscent of Militant in the 1980s, a group which was proscribed by the National Executive Committee of the Labour Party in 1991.

The Labour Party began to reflect the challenges of democracy. Winning in whichever way that is defined should not mean that the 'winner' takes all. In the end, that only leads to intolerance and extremism on all sides. There must be some healing of divisions. Jeremy Corbyn was not the leader to do this. In every constituency, Momentum took their lead from him and his sectarian approach to politics. It was not very pleasant.

After the election I supported legislation and policies I thought were right. I suppose that is how I squared my Labour values with not supporting the policy positions of the leadership. This was very much reflected in my voting record on membership of the EU. I concentrated my attention on my backbench work and particularly around issues concerning children and young people. However, my thoughts returned again and again to the untenability of my position. It was increasingly clear that Jeremy Corbyn would lead the party into the next election.

The Aftermath of the 2017 General Election held on the 8 June

The Conservatives lost their majority and were forced to rely on a Confidence and Supply arrangement with 10 DUP Northern Irish MPs. Despite predictions to the contrary, the Labour Party did much better than expected, which consolidated Jeremy Corbyn's position as Labour Party.

Salisbury and Russia

Mike Gapes: In March 2018 we had the Salisbury poisonings by the nerve agent Novichok, which were quickly linked by our intelligence services to the Russian GRU. I was disgusted by Corbyn's unpatriotic response. He preferred to believe the word of Putin rather than our own services. I praised Theresa May for her statement in the Commons and asked her to seek advice from former Prime Minister Tony Blair.

Chris Leslie: The 2018 local elections were pretty bad for Labour. It looked as though, and particularly after the Salisbury poison attack, that Corbyn was shambolic on national security. Anti-Semitism started to creep up, because there was this hard-left "world view" on the Marxist conspiratorial side of the left, which views everything to do with America as inherently evil, and, by association, everything to do with Israel is evil, and that bled into an anti-Jewish, anti-Semitic approach that was festering away in those ideological corners of the Labour Party and, unfortunately, Corbyn was fairly relaxed about that. The suspicion was that he was always semi-sympathetic to an anti-Israeli, anti-American worldview, and that began to simmer as a problem for him.

Mike Gapes: In a debate on 6 September 2018 I said, *"In my opinion, Mr Seumas Milne has been dissembling and attempting to divert attention from the real cause and the real culprits: the Putin regime in Moscow. Perhaps that should not come as any surprise, because this is the man who hosted President Putin at the Valdai forum in Sochi. This is the man who said in* The Guardian *on 4 March 2015, under the headline, 'The demonisation of Russia risks paving the way for war', that the events in Ukraine were justifiable from the Russian perspective."*

I went on to say, *"That goes against the whole basis of the historic Labour tradition of standing up to the aggression that came from the Soviet Union in the cold war period, our establishment of NATO under Clem Attlee's government, and the consistent support for our values and for the defence of our society by successive Labour Governments. I believe very strongly that the Labour Party would be in a much better place, and that we would have much greater clarity on foreign affairs matters if we had people working for our party leadership who actually believed in those Labour values."* Following my speech, Shadow Foreign Secretary Emily Thornberry came up to me as we were leaving the Chamber and criticised me for attacking Milne since he was a "party official". As I told her at the time, *"Some party officials are more important than others."*

After the 2017 General Election

Chris Leslie: The media were quite happy to have a hung Parliament because it made things more interesting. Theresa May was a weakened figure, and we had another couple of years of Brexit rolling through, which got worse and worse because the Labour Party wasn't really willing to do anything. The members were never going to shift. Moderate members were in despair; I certainly was. For the sake of the country more than anything else. The PLP would meet and would do things occasionally, rebel on certain things. For example, about 60 or 70 of the PLP insisted on trying to retain our membership of the Customs Union, in November 2017, and a big rebellion took place. During that time there were lots of rebellions in the Commons, lots of efforts to do things contrary to the leadership line, but it was clear that nothing was really going to shake this modern Marxist grip on the party.

Mike Gapes: In 2018 the Brexit disaster was dominating everything in Parliament, sucking out all our imagination and energy. I had been very active in trying to stop it. I was one of only 20 Labour MPs to attend the first huge People's Vote march in London on 23 June. But another issue, anti-Semitism, was causing huge dissent with Corbyn inside the PLP. Within the Birthday Club WhatsApp group at that time, opinions were divided on what to do.

By 2018, things were coming to a head, and it was clear that decisions were being made and that actions would have to follow.

Chris Leslie: It was at this point, in the spring of 2018, that some of us asked, "Where are we going with all this?" It was not just a question of our careers within the Labour Party being in abeyance, it was what would happen if this leadership team somehow managed to take over the country, and what damage they would wreak; it would be similar to the divisions that they had created in the Labour Party, and it was just something alien to us. We didn't believe in it, and we didn't want to see it happen, and that was the point at which people like Chuka Umunna, who I was sharing an office with at the time (after I'd been unceremoniously defenestrated from my other office by John McDonnell back in 2015!), started to seriously discuss what to do. We were talking about these things in our "Birthday Club" WhatsApp group. We'd been fairly discreet about it, and totally discreet regarding the MPs who didn't want to stick their necks out too far. We've protected their identities quite faithfully to this day.

The "Birthday Club", Spring 2018

Mike Gapes: In the spring of 2018, I was approached by a Labour MP, who I knew well (I will not name him because he is still in Parliament and has an important role in Keir Starmer's team). He told me that a group within the Birthday Club had been involved in discussions about whether the game was over, and the Labour Party was finished for ever. That chimed very much with my own thinking, and I agreed to join this group. A few days later I was contacted by Gavin Shuker MP. He told me that some Labour MPs had met for discussions around Westminster and a small group had already met for an away day.

I subsequently attended two overnight meetings on a Thursday evening and Friday morning at Fair Oak Farm in Sussex. On each occasion, there were about 15 Labour MPs present. We had very intensive and good discussions there. But no decisions were made at that time. Several of those at Fair Oak Farm who subsequently decided to stay with the Labour Party are now on Keir Starmer's front bench team.

My diary entry on 29 July 2018 summed up my thoughts, *"I have been involved in discussions with a small group of Labour MPs about how and when to split away to form a new independent Labour group. I can't talk to anyone locally or in the family about it. The issue is now coming to a head over antisemitism in our party. Two of my political friends, Margaret Hodge (my neighbour in Barking), and Ian Austin MP for Dudley, are facing disciplinary action by the new Ex-Militant General Secretary Jennie Formby. And the PLP will vote on 5 September to adopt the international definition (IHRA) rather than the watered-down version which is designed to let Corbyn's foul BDS and Palestine Solidarity Trot mates off the hook."* I also suggested there might be a split in the Tories over Brexit and added, *"the current party alignment is not fit for purpose."* I wrote *"A crunch is coming. It will be a real wrench for me to break with 50 years in this party and to fall out with all my friends locally. But I have to be true to myself... I know that I won't be able to stand for election again if Corbyn is the leader, unless I run as an Independent, which would be very hard to do in Ilford South."*

I came back from holiday in France in late August very angry about Corbyn and anti-Semitism. I vented on the Birthday Club WhatsApp, *"I am not prepared to support the racist anti-Semite. Period. It's over for me."*

At this point there was a leak from the WhatsApp group that precipitated a faster response.

Mike Gapes: There had never been any leaks from what I had assumed was a secure WhatsApp group, but someone in that group decided, maliciously I assume, to give that to Lucy Fisher of *The Times*. I told her, *"I don't comment on leaks, all I can say is that I'm very unhappy with Corbyn and I'm agonising every day about my position."* Once *The Times* published the story on the Saturday morning, all hell broke out. I was being pursued by journalists all weekend. I refused about 30 media requests. *The Sun* and *The Daily Mail*, who I didn't speak to, both ran stories based upon what *The Times* had reported but went further by saying I was going to leave the Labour Party.

When Parliament returned for its September sitting, several MPs came up to me to express concern at the leak and give me support. One of them was Chris Leslie, who said to me, "Don't go on your own, there's more of us who are going to be doing this."

"Mike Gapes to resign as MP"?

Mike Gapes: Frank Field had already chosen, in that week, to go Independent. Some newspapers published photos of 10 or 12 MPs who were the most likely suspects to leave, based on Frank Field and me going. Then my local newspaper, the *Ilford Recorder*, picking up the story from the national papers, without contacting me, put on their website *"Mike Gapes to resign as MP"*, (not to leave the Labour Party, but to resign as MP!). It was the August Bank Holiday Weekend. So, I couldn't get hold of the *Ilford Recorder*. I didn't manage to speak to them until the Tuesday morning after the Bank Holiday. I gave them an interview explaining that I had not and would not be resigning as the MP. Then the London Evening Standard picked up what I'd said to the *Ilford Recorder*. I decided had to speak to them. Their report on August 31 said:

"Mr Gapes indicated his decision on whether to stay or go could depend on whether the party's National Executive Committee agrees to adopt in full the internationally agreed definition of anti-Semitism at a showdown meeting on Tuesday. He warned he could not accept any compromise that involved a 'weasel-worded caveat' being adopted at the same time

as the formal definition. 'I am agonising every day about the situation...I will make my own decision about how I deal with this in my own time.' Next week is important because of the NEC [National Executive Committee] on Tuesday and the vote of the Parliamentary Labour Party on Wednesday. In his interview, Mr Gapes said that he had always ruled out quitting until the crisis over anti-Semitism engulfed the party under Mr Corbyn's leadership. 'I now feel tainted and sickened about where we are as a party,' he said. 'There are no good options here. After 50 years as a member, Labour is in my DNA'. " The following week, I agreed to be interviewed by Simon Harris, of ITV London to make clear that I was staying on as a Labour MP at that time.

Many turned a blind eye, but eight MPs could not

Chris Leslie: There were between 80 and 90 Labour MPs who had a similar mindset, but sometimes it's easier just to turn a blind eye to certain things, in the hope that the wind will change, and this is what they decided to do.

Ann Coffey: Of those 80 Labour MPs, only 8 left the party in the end.

Chris Leslie: There were enough of us, however, who were really very frightened about what was going to happen to the country if nothing impeded the hard-left populism that had gripped Labour.

Initially "Plan A" was to make the case about policy issues and mainstream values, to stand up and to rebel, to put the country before party, and those were important things to do within the Labour Party. We had to do it in the Commons: speak out on Europe, speak out on Brexit, and certainly on national security, speak out against anti-Semitism, trying to do our best on those issues. It was clear that there was an aggressive, hard-left attempt beginning to bubble up about deselecting Labour MPs who had voiced these questions.

I was getting enormous attacks and personal vitriol at my local party level. A lot of the Socialist Workers Party, AWL, and the Greens and even elsewhere, had joined the Labour Party, and were coming along, deliberately, to party meetings to goad me and other more longstanding members, who'd been around for 30 years in the party, who were appalled at what was happening. The hard-left members who took over locally would pass motions and resolutions attacking local MPs. It was very, very hostile, very uncomfortable.

"What's Plan B?"

Chris Leslie: Lots of us MPs, then said, "Well, look, Plan A isn't working, we need a Plan B, and what does that look like?" We started a conversation, Chuka, Gavin Shuker, obviously, and different people started to have deeper conversations. These people were the ones that went on to form the Independent Group, but there was obviously a wider group than that.

People like Mike Gapes and Ann Coffey, although they were exasperated about the situation from the outset, weren't initially part of what you might call an "organising activist grouping" to drive forward the strategy of Plan B; that wasn't their nature. But they were willing to take a stand and they were certainly brave enough to speak out, but in terms of actually driving ahead with tactics, how we were going to raise money, how we were going to co-ordinate, a group of us began to form and work through those issues in detail. *"Are we going to take action in a particular and a different way? And what? We have to do something."* The people asking these questions were in that slightly smaller group.

Away Days, Spring and Summer 2018

Chris Leslie: We had "away days". Gavin Shuker arranged for us to go to a little farmhouse in Sussex, Fair Oak Farm, in the spring of 2018. We went again in the summer. Somehow, this second one was leaked to the *Daily Express*, and it was then all over the newspapers: "A bunch of Labour MPs had gone out to basically talk about what on earth is Plan B?" We tried our best to downplay things publicly, but they were very emotional occasions. We all realised that potentially we were going to facilitate the advent of a group of people to power who we fundamentally disagreed with; what a strange position that was to find yourself in. You were a Labour MP, you were going to be counted, in our constitution, automatically, as giving your assent to Corbyn and McDonnell and Diane Abbott and Richard Burgon or whoever, as taking over the levers of power as

Secretaries of State, and you would be party to that. Unconscionable.

The "When" WhatsApp Group, Autumn 2018

Mike Gapes: By the autumn of 2018, I was pretty clear in my own mind that I was going to do something dramatic, whether it was just to announce that I was retiring, or whether it was to say I couldn't support Corbyn at the next election. I had made up my mind that I could not stand again as a Corbyn Labour candidate. Then in early November 2018 a group of us decided to set up a separate WhatsApp group called "When". The "When" group began detailed discussions about, well, if we do have a plan B, when do we do it and what does it involve? And what are the reasons why people are going to leave?

"Are we going to form a different group and sit separately?"

Chris Leslie: The 2017 election had been bad enough in that respect, but it was clear that the next one could be even closer and there was always an outside risk that Corbyn could actually be elected. There was no excuse of un-electability, really, any longer, and that's why we felt a really heavy duty on our shoulders to do something, and that was the point at which we started the conversation about, *"Well, are we going to just wait to get deselected? Or are we going to step ahead of that and create something that can shine a spotlight on all this?"* We knew we had to do two things: shine that spotlight on what was wrong with Corbyn and the hard-left worldview, so that the country at least paid attention to it; second, find a way of offering some alternative in the centre-ground space, the progressive centre-left. That's where the idea came, *"Well, are we going to have to leave and form a different group and sit separately?"* Obviously, we knew in reality that we would be sacrificing our time and politics and Parliament and our careers and so forth, and what would that involve? Emotionally, socially, career-wise, all those other things, what would it involve?

CHAPTER SIX

Reasons for Leaving

"I did what I thought was right"

In reality, there weren't that many different reasons for leaving their parties. It is important to remember that these were people who had been members of their parties for between 32 and 50 years; the decision to leave cannot have been easy.

Joan Ryan: As someone who had the occasional, perfectly amicable, dealings with Jeremy Corbyn as a fellow north London MP, I was nonetheless fully aware of his obstinacy, rigidity and his self-perception. The problem we have all confronted over the now past years is that this is a man whose belief in his own moral rectitude means that he is unable to brook any criticism. Jeremy's absolute certainty about his impeccable anti-racism credentials makes it totally impossible for him to accept that any of his actions could possibly have led to the anti-Semitism crisis Labour confronts. But without such recognition, real change is impossible.

Corbyn presided over a culture of intolerance, abuse and bullying in his party. His hard-left political machine sought to crush and silence dissent. It repeatedly broke the party's own rules to further its interests, and it treated those with whom the leader disagreed as traitors who should be driven out of the party. This is unsurprising: Corbyn was and is surrounded by a clique of Marxists and Trotskyites who do not believe in parliamentary democracy, pluralism or the rule of law. The prospect of these individuals getting into Downing Street was truly frightening, and a danger the likes of which this country has not experienced in modern times.

Labour has always been a broad church and it has been led from the left before, but Corbyn and his allies had a project to convert Labour into a far-left party. They had operated in a grey zone between the fringes of Labour and the hard left for decades. This was their opportunity to bring the "outside" left into the Labour Party and to change it beyond recognition. Were my disagreements with the Labour leadership simply about its timid and cynical stance on Brexit? I may have stayed longer to fight for my beliefs from inside the party, but to me anti-Jewish racism isn't an issue upon which we can compromise. It's not something you negotiate around, or something you agree to disagree about. It's a moral absolute and you can't trade it off against other priorities. I did not believe Labour could or would change while Jeremy Corbyn was leading it.

Corbyn has been a uniquely divisive Labour leader. His MPs tried to unseat him less than a year into his leadership. His Shadow Cabinet lacked talent and intellect because it was overwhelmingly drawn from a narrow element of the parliamentary party, and his own office was, according to his head of policy, characterised by a "lack of professionalism, competence and human decency". Corbyn has spent much of his political life doing little more than addressing adoring crowds of like-minded hard-left activists. When he has at last tried to run something – the Labour Party – he has shown none of the managerial competence, decision-making abilities or team-building skills that one would expect in a Prime Minister.

I knew that Jeremy Corbyn was utterly unfit to be Prime Minister. His record as Labour leader offered a frightening preview as to the kind of government he would lead. First, he tolerated anti-Jewish racism. From BNP leader Nick Griffin, and the former Ku Klux Klan head, David Duke, to an assorted bunch of Holocaust-deniers, terrorist-sympathisers and Jew-haters, Corbyn appears to attract the most unsavoury supporters. When anti-Semites flooded into the Labour Party after he became leader in 2015, Corbyn's reaction was one of denial, indifference and foot-dragging. Many of my Jewish constituents, friends and former parliamentary colleagues were understandably anxious and upset about the prospect of such a man becoming Prime Minister. So, too, was I.

Chris Leslie: The context of my exasperation was the maddening self-indulgence of the party turning its back on the real world and the wider public.

The preference was for an ideological extravagance for years with a leadership not just alien to the electorate but wrong for office. Corbyn got elected, essentially with that populist appeal to the members, and those recruited from the Socialist Workers' Party and other extremes.

Ann Coffey: There were many who shared the same despair about the direction of the party and the shameful failure to deal with anti-Semitism, who thought that they 'should stay and fight'. Some people believed that if the Labour Party got hammered in the next general election, then that would create change and, to some extent, they were right, because the party did get hammered and Jeremy's gone. It would have been better for the people of this country if Jeremy Corbyn had gone before the election and we had had a new *leader* more acceptable to the public. It is the overriding responsibility of a leader of a political party to win power for that party in a parliamentary democracy. The Labour Party was formed to offer an alternative for working people; a party that would be able to bring in legislation to improve working and social conditions and opportunities for education by winning seats in elections and forming a government.

Joan Ryan: It was clear that a Corbyn government would do serious harm to Britain's social cohesion and the fabric of our society. Its agenda is riddled with a divisive "them-and-us" populism. Many of the hard-left fanatics it selected to fight key seats epitomise this agenda.

Among them are people who fantasise about the death of former Prime Ministers and boast about their plans to celebrate these historic events. Other such individuals maintain social media accounts dripping with misogyny, anti-Semitism and homophobia. There were even prospective MPs who would belittle the Holocaust and spread fantastical 9/11 conspiracy theories. Under any previous leader, such people would have been kicked out of the party, not chosen as parliamentary candidates. Yet it says much about Corbyn's debased values that he is willing to tolerate, campaign alongside and even see such individuals in Parliament. Like Donald Trump, Corbyn's sole test of a person's morality is their loyalty to him. This is a deeply dangerous trait.

Anna Soubry: It wasn't just a rejection of my party that had helped me to get elected to Parliament, it was actually a rejection about the way that we had done politics for too long and then a recognition and acceptance that we now had to do politics differently and better. It really was about doing things differently, and that perhaps, gets a bit lost in all of this, because it wasn't just about the state of the Tory Party, the state of the Labour Party, it was a genuine desire to do things differently, which is why we talked about doing politics on a collaborative basis, on a more cross-party basis. It was about developing an evidence-based policy, which was hugely important to me as I had worked as a lawyer for many years. It was also about doing politics that genuinely engaged with real people and that represented their real concerns. It was also about being brave enough and bold enough to lead people towards a destination they may not have originally wanted to go to, or even agree with initially. A fundamental role of anybody in politics is to make an argument and make the case and win the argument and win people's minds. How else do you get elected in a marginal seat? You only get elected in a marginal seat if you persuade enough people not to vote the way they did last time, but to vote a different way this time. You persuade them by example, and by argument. How do you ever make all the great changes that we've made, whether it's in race relations legislation, whether it's in sexual discrimination legislation, rights for women, rights for gay people, equal pay; if you just looked at opinion polls, you probably, you wouldn't do those things. But you believe something is right, and then you make your case, and you persuade people, and you do it because you're brave enough to do it, because you believe it's the right thing to do for the common good, for the good of the people, for the good of the country to lead, to win over hearts and minds. It seems that we have seen this almost being obliterated in British politics nowadays, where too many people are more concerned about what the focus groups tell us, and what the *Daily Mail* headline will be? As opposed to saying, "No, we do this because we believe it's the right thing to do."

One of the things I did find quite interesting in my time in the People's Vote, when I got to know a lot of people from the Labour Party, was too many of them had lost the ability to be big and brave and principled. We would sit, and we would have an idea about something, and immediately it was, *"Well, I think we should test it on a focus group."* I'd sit there and, at times, I would say, *"Guys, what do you think?",* and the response would be, *"Well, you know, let's test it on"* – *"No, no, what do you think? Do you think that's a good idea, a bad idea? Have a view, have an opinion."* Now, can I just counter all of this, because this is all about the balances that have to exist in a good political system? The danger in that view is ending up in a country that does what its politicians believe without taking the people with them.

Joan Ryan: Anyone who has been involved in politics knows how tribal our party system is. Despite our internal disagreements – many of them heated – our loyalties are akin to those some people feel to their football team or, rather more profoundly, their religion or family. Leaving the Labour Party was terribly difficult in many ways. Relationships – both locally and nationally – are altered very suddenly and dramatically. These are people I've fought alongside over issues I and they care about very deeply. At the same time, realising that I had to leave the Labour Party and stand with the Jewish community was, perhaps, the easiest decision of my life. I knew I could not remain in a party that I regarded as institutionally anti-Semitic.

Labour was once a patriotic party, clear-eyed about the threats to Britain's national security and committed to opposing them; Corbyn undermined this completely. He steered the party towards his own warped 'anti-imperialist' worldview: disreputable support towards ballot-stuffing South American leftists; a barely concealed sympathy for the gay-hating, terror-supporting ayatollahs in Tehran, and, most worryingly of all, he displayed a total failure to recognise the danger posed to Britain and our European allies by Vladimir Putin's Russia. Indeed, when Putin's henchmen launched a chemical weapons attack in Salisbury, Labour's first response was to seek to muddy the waters by casting aspersions on the findings of Britain's world-leading intelligence services.

Defending the nation's security is the most important duty of any government. Corbyn would have abandoned our allies, and appeased our enemies, to pursue a reckless foreign policy driven by far-left prejudice. He would not act in Britain's national interest.

The Prime Minister carries awesome responsibilities with huge powers at his or her disposal. Jeremy Corbyn was incapable of discharging the former and should never be allowed to get his hands on the latter. Doing everything possible to prevent him from walking into 10 Downing Street on the day after a general election was an absolute necessity.

Mike Gapes: For me, it wasn't just the anti-Semitism, although the anti-Semitism issue was important, and it wasn't just Brexit. For me, the most important thing was the general foreign policy;

Putin and Russia, NATO, anti-Americanism, support for Hamas and Hezbollah, cosying up to all kinds of dodgy regimes, Corbyn had been the President of the "Stop the West" coalition and his Leaders Office was inhabited by people who had that kind of politics. The idea of Seumas Milne being in Number 10, directing Foreign Office Diplomats as to what position we would take on the international crisis involving Russia, filled me with horror.

Joan Ryan: The problem is compounded by a still greater one: that anti-Zionism – shaped by a broader, anti-western, perverted form of post-colonial far-left politics – is absolutely central to the Corbyn worldview. As I alluded to in my resignation statement, his determination in the summer of 2018 – despite the potential political cost and damage – to push for the right of anti-Semites to describe Israel as a "racist endeavour" is testament to how deep his commitment to anti-Zionism truly is.

Anna Soubry: I used to look at people and think I genuinely don't know what I've got in common with you, politically, I just don't. And you're – I'm in the same party as you. I mean, that is some broad church. But of course, it isn't a broad church anymore.

I think if we'd ever had the opportunity to challenge how we did politics, I think I would've shaken my Conservative colleagues up a bit as well, because I think there was a danger that some of them were still stuck in the old ways of how you connect with real people and how you make sure that you don't lose them in your desire to make the changes that you want. Some of them would have found some of my views a bit challenging, because it's about doing politics in a different way, and part of that is the tribal party thing, that I do notice far more in the Labour Party than in the Conservative Party.

Chris Leslie: As well as talking about Brexit, occasionally you would have very dark conversations about, *"Oh, God, our party is terrible. Isn't it awful? We're in such a state,"* and they would say back, *"Oh, you think your party's bad? You know, ours is much worse."* We would have these, sort of, you know, comparisons of woe from the summer of 2018. You would find yourself sharing platforms with people, finding you had more in common with them than your own party members and some of your own front bench. There was a sort of natural evolution of where things were going. We didn't particularly share every aspect of our decision to leave the Labour Party with those Conservatives, but they had a fair inkling that something was going on.

Anna Soubry: If we were to sit people down in a room and go through it all, with that wing of the Labour Party and that wing of the Conservative Party, you'd find that we have more in common than we don't have in common; I've always thought that. I think that's a critical thing and people tried to make the same analogy with the SDP and to look back, and, of course, people found that they agreed from different positions but there were never really any big Tories who ever came over. In our case, it was more that they agreed on so much politically; we actually wanted to do things differently.

Ann Coffey: I had made up my mind to leave but I wanted that to be more than an individual act. I had been talking to various people within the Parliamentary Labour Party, over a series of months; people who felt like me. We talked about the idea of leaving as a group, of trying to do something worthwhile when leaving the party, offering another option to people; something that was not the Labour Party or the Conservative Party. It wasn't about finding a "middle", it was about working out a different relationship with the public, not one based on distrust and disrespect, but with policies that were solutions to 21st-century issues and free of the baggage of the past.

Anna Soubry: There are some people, of course, who would say, *"Ah, but I did do what I thought was the right thing."* And even though you might say, *"But you went a different route, you changed your mind,"* but I did what I thought was right. And actually, they do live with themselves, they can justify it and they can look back at themselves in the mirror. But if you're a politician and can't be true to what you believe in and do what you believe is the right thing, then we're absolutely doomed. You know, it's even more important, and, you know, you do look, and whatever your politics are, you look at the House of Commons, and there are, too many people who are there and they're just very happy to have a nice easy life. If you want a nice easy life, you don't go into bloody politics, for crying out loud. There's a big difference between an easy life and working hard but some people don't see that. "Well, I work very hard," they say; *"Yeah, I know you work very hard, I'm not saying you don't. But you always take the easy option."*

Joan Ryan: In leaving a Labour Party poisoned by prejudice against Jewish people and overwhelmed by fear and hatred, I felt I was doing what I'd always tried to encourage children to do: to stand up for what you believe in and never give up.

Anna Soubry: If you'd looked at same-sex marriage, which is a really good example; if you'd done what others did, and particularly in my constituency, you'd have said, "Oh, my postbag is full of people who are against it so I'm going to vote against it." What I said to myself was, "Well, I believe in equal marriage, I'm going to have public meetings and argue for it in my email newsletter and local media. I'm going to go broader than the people that are part of a campaign group that write to me, and I'm going to say to my constituents: This is why I support it, but I want to know what you think." When I did that, it was amazing, because, actually, the majority of emails I got did support equal marriage, but even if they hadn't, I would have voted for it, because I believed in it. Legislation can lead to a change in the public's attitudes.

The Race Relations Act is a very good example of where, if you'd decided whether to legislate based on an opinion poll, you'd probably have found most people didn't want to outlaw racial discrimination, though they're always dependent on the questions you ask. But politicians who voted for that legislation did so because they believed it was the right thing to do. We suffer profoundly from not having people like that amongst our leaders in politics today; people who do things because they believe in it, because they have a set of principles and they have a set of beliefs. You've got to have people with principles, who'll be brave and lead. You know, you should get elected on the basis that I have principles and I will be true to these principles, and I will be courageous, and I will be brave. I'm not a delegate, I'm a representative, but I'm also an elected politician, I'm not just there to trot through a lobby. I'm also there to do brave things, which might be controversial and which you might not agree with at the time, because otherwise we get that diminution that has led to populism. That's the rise of Trump and it's the rise of Boris Johnson, and it's so incredibly dangerous. We have the perfect example at the moment of us putting in place some measures, some very onerous measures, in relation to when people come into this country. This mandatory quarantine for any returning Brit, people returning from a holiday or a trip abroad, and there is no argument or scientific evidence to support this; the government's doing it for no other reason, apparently, than that it is popular. I would lay very good money that somebody's done a focus group, and they've said, "So, what about people from abroad?" "Oh, foreigners coming in with their disease, they've brought it in." Therefore, they will — oh, put them in quarantine. I bet nobody's said to them, "Oh, no, actually, it's you returning from your summer holiday, you will be in quarantine," because you can bet your life that's not popular. I really do believe this.

Chris Leslie: In truth, we were leaving the Labour Party for a series of principles. It wasn't just anti-Semitism. It wasn't just national security. For me, it was also very much about their approach to the economy, their dislike of business, and, by association, dislike of the European Union, and that Corbyn and McDonnell were just the wrong people to run the country. My main objective was always to shine a spotlight on why they weren't fit and proper individuals to take office in government. Frankly, if I was going to be leaving politics because we'd reached the end of the road trying to save Labour, and sadly exiting in that way, I would do all that I could to bring them down with me, to be honest. And in many respects, we did succeed in that, if you step back with today's perspective. Certain things needed to be said, and I was damned if the hard left were going to get away with a free pass, and a free run into government. Something had to be done. I was well aware that, beyond impeding Corbyn, it was quite a different thing altogether to expect a realignment of British politics as well! We had a good attempt at doing it, and the Independent Group was very well received, initially. We quickly had other MPs spontaneously mirror what we had done: Joan Ryan left the next day. Ian Austin left, although he had a different view on Brexit, so didn't join us. John Woodcock had already left the Labour Party, for different reasons in the summer, and was sitting as Independent. There were various Labour MPs sitting as Independents.

Anna Soubry: Then you get into the classic example of that, that is our immigration policy. Our immigration policy in support of the free movement of people led to a significant increase of migrant workers from EU countries, Romania and Lithuania under the Blair government, but the argument wasn't being made out on the doorstep with people as to why this was a good thing. Issues like immigration, which are prone to emotional argument rather than fact, need big and brave politicians making the arguments for and against.

Things haven't changed. I remember a conversation with David Lammy in, I think 2016, just after the referendum; I didn't know David at this time. He was a bit suspicious of me because I was a Tory, but we soon got on very well. He said to me, "Do you know what, I reckon you and I are the only two Members of Parliament who actually have the courage to stand up in Parliament, in public, and make the positive case for immigration." At that time, he was right, and I think that speaks volumes. I always remember being really shocked and actually very saddened at the number of otherwise very honourable Labour Members of Parliament, who, I felt, instead of standing and engaging in that argument and actually making the case, would acquiesce to the argument on the doorstep. When somebody said, "Oh, we've got all these foreigners here, you know, we've got too many immigrants," or whatever, and I've had that from constituents, I would say, "Really, where, where are they?" I'd look round and I'd go, "Really, where are they? Do you know how many Black people there are or immigrants, because they are different? Did you know that they're different?" You have start to have this conversation. "Do you know how many there are in Broxtowe?" You know, it was about 2% actually. You start to have a conversation – and I'm afraid too many people would, when that thing was said, "We've got too many immigrants" would say, "Oh, I know, I understand, I understand where you're coming from." I don't frigging understand where they are coming from, and sorry, I'm not going to pander to that nonsense. I'm going to – I'd challenge it robustly with facts and argument – and some people you will never persuade, of course. But, in my experience, when you had a proper robust conversation, an exchange of views, put the evidence there, invariably, I could persuade people, and that has, with few exceptions, just has not happened. And so, look where we ended up, in this terrible mess of an immigration policy based on ignorance and ideology. And look where we ended up with a Labour Party that couldn't make the case for free movement, for God's sakes.

And never mind the Conservative Party, because, of course, the direct consequence of all of this was Windrush, with the vans; it's never-ending. People including Boris Johnson didn't even know that if you've got indeterminate leave to remain, you're not entitled to public funds, and so on and so forth; he's clueless. This is all a consequence of a view that "these people" are bad, as opposed to good. I believe that "these people" are great and they contribute to our country in so many ways.

The only good thing to come out of Windrush was that it did make a lot of people realise that immigrants were their neighbours. It really is the person who pays their taxes, who works hard, who actually is really rather brilliant, and despite this we are trying to send them back home. I'd like to think that after every great crisis, there is always a change; that's what history tells us. I don't know what's going to come out of this great crisis, but, if we actually have, through Keir Starmer, the making of the positive case for immigration, the positive case for the huge contribution and that "immigrants" are the people who clean the loos, drive the tubes and the buses, and not just the doctors and the healthcare workers, but actually all the way through our society, at all levels. That will be a positive, because something good has to come out of this and I think people are beginning to see it. Of course, the bloody tragedy is that we've left the European Union, haven't we?

I didn't agree with it; I was mute, and I didn't stand up against it, but the idea that we're going to reduce immigration to tens of thousands was just fucking nonsense, but there we are. They're making promises to get a *Daily Mail* headline.

CHAPTER SEVEN

Launching the Independent Group

"When we left and did the launch on that Monday in February 2019, it was a very big deal."

Chris Leslie: We started kicking around the idea of the Independent Group, which to me was the obvious "holding" name that we would give ourselves. It involved circulating around draft documents setting out our values and our principles. I wrote a long pamphlet on the centre-ground mainstream values in Britain today with the Social Market Foundation; it was probably rather too long, but I just felt I needed to put core principles down in writing. What were my values, and what was I talking about, and why? I was glad I did it, because it definitely helped inform the draft statement of values that I pulled together later on, in consultation with the others. I'm afraid I was quite an activist on these tasks! I felt it was better to be proposing stuff rather than just present blank sheets of paper in meetings. I'm glad that we drafted the Statement of Independence that we had and then presented, because I think those things worked quite well. Certainly, at that time, there were a lot of very tormented, torn individuals in the Parliamentary Labour Party who were very tempted to leave, but we were asking people, really, to give up secure ways of paying their mortgages, and potentially imperil their family income, to cut themselves off from their social circle and their career and prospects and give up a position of apparent authority and respect within the community as an MP, and so forth. In the end the numbers went down, and there were about seven of us who were willing to do that. By the time we got to the launch date in February 2019 we had our number settled, a plan of action, and our statement of values.

Certainly, there were 15 or 20 colleagues who absolutely understood what we were doing and where we were coming from. At the time there were also others who were leaving Parliament, in dribs and drabs, because they'd seen the writing on the wall themselves. The situation wasn't helped by the fact that there was quite a division in what you might call the 'social democratic firmament'.

Tom Watson's "Future Britain Group"

Chris Leslie: There was a separate polarity around Tom Watson, who was persuading people all the lines, *"You don't need to do anything really drastic or difficult. Stick with me. I have a better plan that doesn't involve you putting your neck on the block. We can just hold back."* Team Watson was persuading people not to jump, not to come with us. Certainly, that was the case after we did jump, and Tom Watson set up his "Future Britain Group" the week after we formed The Independent Group. All the remaining Labour MPs and peers went along, – standing room only apparently – putting their hopes in the fact that Tom Watson would solve the problem.

In hindsight, we know that he never did anything of the sort. I think that "Future Britain Group" only met the once; it corralled those who were wavering and helped stop them taking action. He will receive a Peerage and has left Parliament, and a lot of Labour MPs, who had put their hopes in him, definitely felt left in the lurch ahead of the December 2019 election. But to be fair to him, I also understand that he had his anxieties about the tactics, and whether they would succeed, and probably he was in two minds. Was it better to work with Corbyn and hold them close singing, *"Oh, Jeremy Corbyn!"* out of some perceived sense of loyalty and almost smother them? Or to actually stand up publicly, explain to constituents that this was no longer the Labour Party as they knew it, and leave it? I think the difference was that some of us just didn't want to take the risk to the country of Corbyn winning, finding ourselves as Minister for Paperclips or whatever it might be, but in the process, help prop up a government that you just knew was wrong for the country. Most Labour MPs were persuaded to keep their heads down and their mouths shut, and it's very easy to persuade people with a risk-averse option. *"Oh, yeah, I am sympathetic with what you're doing, but I don't want to do it just now. I'll wait, I'll wait."* Some Labour MPs actually said to us, *"If you can prove to us that there is a viable group, that you've got funding and support, and you can make it stand, then we will come with you."* It's a bit chicken-and-egg though, and you'd have these conversations and say to them, *"Well, unless you come with us, it won't work, and the chances of it being viable will be diminished."* The "viability" question definitely played on our minds quite a lot, and we knew this was a long shot, of course it was, always was.

Cross-Party Trips and Closer Affinity

Anna Soubry: What happened was that increasingly, over time, we always knew, there was an elephant in the room on a number of occasions leading up to what happened when people left their political parties. It was quite funny. I remember going on a couple of trips with Chuka and Chris and a couple of other people, who would be horrified to have their names mentioned now, and increasingly, the elephant in the room was suddenly spoken about. I'd say, *"Yeah, but we're all going to get together. We've got to get together. We've got to change things. We should be in the same political party."* Those sorts of conversations do change, and eventually you all begin to talk in the same language, and the elephant is no longer in the room. Suddenly you're talking about it and it's not a question of if, it's when you do this thing. For some of them, to talk in those terms would have been seen like treason of the highest order, whereas, to me, it felt very natural. I never felt unnatural about the whole thing. I just, I felt comfortable, I finally felt comfortable with people, as opposed to sitting and really feeling bristly.

Chris Leslie: The viability issue was actually partly responsible for the conversations we started to have with those disenchanted Conservative MPs, such as Anna Soubry, Heidi Allen and Sarah Wollaston, who were working with us a lot on the rebellions on Brexit. Our grouping of MPs was actually in quite a position of power because we'd managed to co-ordinate a bloc of votes in the Commons that was able to force the pace on certain things like the Customs Union, Single Market, and other issues. The Labour Party felt it had to begrudgingly go along with our rebellious bloc, because that was the only way it would ever win votes in the Commons. We were winning votes and there were some good relationships building with Conservative rebels on the moderate side.

Mike Gapes: Our "When" group had long discussions in November. It was decided that because several of us were very involved in those Brexit debates, we couldn't really do anything before the crucial Brexit votes were held. Those Brexit votes were set for December. But then, Theresa May pulled the plug halfway through the debate on her Withdrawal Agreement just before Christmas. The Bill was then scheduled to come back in January 2019. Our group decided that we had to delay any move until after then. The eight people involved were all clear at that time and were determined we were going, but we weren't sure when. We were now meeting together regularly, and the eight of us were even hiding in plain sight by eating together in the Members Dining Room every Wednesday after Prime

Ministers Questions. We also planned initiatives and debates to challenge Corbyn. One example was the Urgent Question I had on Venezuela where I denounced him and several of his front bench for supporting the repressive Maduro kleptocracy.

The Launch of the Independent Group in 2019

Chris Leslie: When we left and did the launch on that Monday in February 2019, it was a very big deal. Seven of us left Labour (although until that weekend, it was going to be eight of us that were going to do it, but one person changed their mind at the very last minute, who is still in Parliament. We haven't shared that with very many people, but fair enough, it was a big commitment.) Alongside all of this, the anti-Semitism issue had been growing bigger and bigger; in that January in particular, Luciana Berger was getting more and more abuse from her local party. They passed a resolution condemning her and that was particularly potent in the media; here was a young pregnant woman being harassed in her own party, which became a sort of tipping-point issue. We were also conscious that she was going to have a baby at some point in March, so we knew that in terms of timing, if we were ever going to do this, it had to be then. There was some talk of doing it before the September 2018 Party Conference, or around that time, but it just didn't feel like the right moment for it, and I don't think Luciana was ready to do it at that point. By then everybody had made their minds up, that we were going to do it. There was a lot of preparatory work: preparing, thinking what we were going to do, what sort of values we would talk about. We were even thinking about what a grid of events and interventions look like in the subsequent days. We knew that when we launched this sort of thing, it would be a really hard thing to do within the British system. You can see this in the modern day; somebody sticks their neck out and says something, and then there's a great vat of cynicism poured all over it straightaway; that is just the nature of the British system, really.

Mike Gapes: Although others might not have realised it, I felt I was pulling my punches, inhibited in saying what I really thought. In late January, Luciana Berger made it very clear that she wanted us to go before she went on maternity leave in mid-February. Luciana was central to the fight against the anti-Semitism of Corbyn Labour, and we hoped other MPs would join us if she left. So, we agreed to set a deadline for all of us. We finally decided we would go before the February school half-term recess. There was growing media speculation, but we managed to keep our decision and timing secret. But then events intervened again, as the February recess was cancelled because of Brexit.

So, we actually went on Monday 18 February when Parliament was sitting. Just days before we left, one of our group got cold feet and changed his mind. He had been, ironically, the person who approached me and had got me into those early Fair Oak Farm discussions a year before, but now I was leaving the Labour Party and he was not. I was never entirely sure why he had changed his mind, but I understood how difficult the decision to leave was for all of us, for we had parents, partners, families, friends and residual loyalties to our Labour values. It was still not easy for me to do this. So, there were now seven of us in the end. We meticulously prepared our launch. We worked out the seating and speaking order which had to be changed at short notice now we were seven and not eight. We held a run-through rehearsal on the Sunday afternoon at a building near Trafalgar Square, and then gathered a 7am on Monday morning at the old County Hall Hotel on the South Bank. The media were sent an email from Chuka Umunna's office to inform them of an important announcement at 10am. No details or names were given. We were determined to get the maximum impact. And we did, as one by one, seven Labour MPs, Luciana Berger, Chuka Umunna, Chris Leslie, Ann Coffey, Angela Smith, Gavin Shuker and myself walked up to the platform in a packed, hot, small room filled with journalists and TV crews, to resign from the Labour Party and establish The Independent Group. Our presentations were very good, and the event and subsequent media questions went well. I myself did 28 interviews that day, and my colleagues were in similar demand. Our ranks were soon joined when Joan Ryan, who hadn't been in our discussions at all, telephoned Chris Leslie that evening, and she came to join us the next day.

Joan Ryan at the opening of the Hub in her constituency

Joan Ryan: By 19 February 2019, I had concluded that
              while my values hadn't changed those of the
              Labour Party had. I resigned from Labour that
              day and left the party of which I'd been a
              member for more than 40 years and which I'd
              been proud to serve as a councillor, MP and
              government minister. I hit the news with my
              resignation from Labour on the Tuesday night
              around 10pm, and it ran big throughout
              Wednesday morning. The timing was
              significant in that less than 48 hours earlier
              seven former Labour colleagues left Labour to
              become the Independent Group, I left on my
              own and then joined these brave colleagues. I
              knew too that I planned to speak in a House of
              Commons debate the very next day on anti-
              Semitism and felt I could not simply repeat the
              criticisms I had made previously of the Labour
              leadership. This was a time for action not
              simply for more words.

Chris Leslie: On the Wednesday of that week, our Conservative friends decided that they would join us and do the same. That is where it became really interesting, fusing together the three Conservatives, who'd left predominantly for Brexit, but also, really underlying that their party was moving to the right-wing fringe. Our party had moved to the left-wing fringe and there was this vacuum in the centre ground, and maybe this was the spark of something that could have that conversation. I do think there was a massive amount of public goodwill behind us; they knew what we were doing, and why we had come to these sets of decisions. Over the course of the next few weeks, we had something like 15,000 individual members of the public donating small sums of money to our fighting; there was a lot of support out there for us, and we ended up with about 100,000 people on our mailing list after the first month or so. It was big and it was growing, and it was certainly bigger than Momentum at one point as they never got to that level on social media etc. We also had more followers on our Twitter feed. It was a big deal.

Mike Gapes: Then three women MPs from the Conservatives, who Chuka had been involved in talking to about Brexit, decided to leave their party and join us. They knew there was a group of Labour MPs who were unhappy, but they didn't know who we were or when we were going or what we were doing, unlike us they had made no plans or preparations, so with our assistance they hurriedly put together a press event on Wednesday

20 February at One Great George Street. We had been 7, now we were 11. We were at that time very optimistic that other MPs, might now join us. I had several warm, friendly conversations with Labour MPs wishing me well. Reaction to our departure was interesting. Shadow Foreign Secretary Emily Thornberry and others were denouncing us for leaving as traitors, scum and scabs. In contrast, Labour Deputy Leader Tom Watson was saying, "They've raised serious concerns, we need to take account of what they're saying." His approach was very much to try and shore up, to stop other people leaving. Tom set up a group inside the Parliamentary Labour Party, designed deliberately to keep people in. Many in the PLP were waiting for Tom to move against Corbyn, which, of course, never happened. Instead, Tom Watson was outmanoeuvred by Momentum owner Jon Lansman over the summer and ended up standing down at the general election.

Chris Leslie: We had our launch, and it was actually incredibly successful. I remember having to ring up Laura Kuenssberg on the Sunday night to say: "I'm *so sorry, I know it's the school half term"*, but we had to tip the key journalists off so they'd attend, and it was partly that we chose that week because Parliament wasn't sitting. We knew that the other Labour front benchers would not be around or co-ordinated, so we thought that gave us a bit of an element of surprise. We called all the journalists to come to County Hall, which we'd hired for our launch. We had to get there for 6:00am, and it was a very nervous time. We had met the night before to do a little dress rehearsal. The next morning, we sat down and planned the choreography meticulously: who was going to speak and in what running order. It's such a good thing to have done because it made the event run far smoother on that Monday morning. My wife, Nicola, who volunteered to help with co-ordinating many of the policy and operational aspects, was closely involved throughout and so we had a full family commitment to this exercise!

At the County Hall venue, we gathered in front of a big crowd of media and reporters, each said our piece, which was quite difficult to do publicly, and launched our Independent Group. Then we went and did our follow-up media. Unfortunately, there were a few things that went awry straightaway.

Anna Soubry: I think it was the sight of them going into that press conference and there was something very powerfully symbolic about Luciana, I think, standing there, heavily pregnant. A woman looks quite magnificent when she's in those final stages of her pregnancy, because you're like a magnificent, sort of, galleon, and statuesque, but also, there's an incredible vulnerability, as well. Luciana does have a look. I mean, she's just very striking, and this woman's standing there with all that magnificence, but also the vulnerability, saying, you know, "I have left the Labour Party, because I've been hounded out because I'm Jewish." I just think that that, subconsciously and consciously, just smacked people right between the eyes. I think that was hugely significant. People did have huge hope when three Tories left, that we were going to do something new; maybe one day it will happen, but sadly, it wasn't to be then; sadly, I might be a bit too old now, but I will do what I can to help.

Mike Gapes: After our launch events, there followed an intensive period, trying to build on what we'd already agreed. The original 7 of us had agreed a statement of values in advance of our launch. We had worked closely together for some months. But now we had been joined by three people who came from a different political culture with very different experiences. I had known Anna Soubry, but not well, I had spoken to Sarah Wollaston once or twice, but I had never had a conversation with Heidi Allen. Now we were in the same political group. All that united us was a common opposition to Labour and Tory extremism, and to Brexit.

Chris Leslie and Mike Gapes campaigning
outside Waterloo Station in the elections for the
European Parliament in May 2019.

Chris Leslie: We had some heady days in the early phases.
There was a lot of interest in what we were
doing, and an independent group was a novel
concept. We had a grid of events in our first
week plan, including our inaugural meeting
where Gavin Shuker was chosen as our
Convenor. We had to pick somebody to setup
and chair meetings, and I realised that we
needed a basic constitution, so we drafted one.
I was always reluctant to have discussions with
totally blank pieces of paper because we needed
to progress and we needed to move forward; if
we stood still, I was worried we were going to
wither and disappear. Unfortunately, we soon
realised that the Electoral Commission in the
UK were a very, very restrictive organisation;

you can't just stand for elections, you have to jump through a number of their hoops to be registered as a political party. We were conscious that the local elections were coming up in May, but we weren't really ready, because we didn't have a party nationwide, so we didn't intend to stand in those. We hadn't registered a name of a political party and such. Meanwhile, what started to happen in Parliament was that there were real opportunities to impede Theresa May's Brexit deal. Ironically, because we were rebelling so much, and succeeding in our rebellion, so she kept falling into difficulties, and in March, of course, she failed to secure Parliamentary authority for her Withdrawal Bill. I think it was her third time and she felt that we couldn't be clear that we were going to withdraw from the European Union on her schedule. She reluctantly had to accept that the country would need to proceed with a European Parliamentary election – not part of the original plan.

Mike Gapes: We intended to develop policies and a new approach. We had lots of ideas about what we were going to do. We were going to have a series of events around the country, thinking, engaging, listening exercises, working towards some kind of membership system, and planned to have our first conference in the autumn. We had intended preparing a policy statement for that. We weren't intending to set up a political party at that stage, it was very much developing a platform for a group of Independent MPs and supporters to work together. But in retrospect we were naïve. This planning was all swept aside by events.

Chris Leslie: They didn't coincide with the local elections, and the group thought, *"Oh my goodness. How can you be a new force in Parliament and in the country for that centre-ground space, particularly when Brexit was the number one issue and be absent from an election?"* Brexit was the greatest issue, it was the only game in town, and could we really not take a stand on these things? The Labour Party was hedging and not really doing or saying anything on the topic. The Liberal Democrats, meanwhile, in the winter of the early phase of 2019, were in a really poor place. They were in single-digit figures in the polls, and they were not thriving. Whereas the Independent Group got up to 18% in the national opinion polls. We were thinking, "If we're going to do this, how can we go through a European election and just, 'sit on our hands' while the old, traditional parties did their thing?" We did have this discussion and it just didn't seem viable to let the elections pass without us moving to the next phase, which was to register as a party. Unfortunately, we weren't able to register the name "Independent Group" because of the ridiculous rules of the Electoral Commission. They said, "You can't use the word 'Independent.'" It was maddening and quite preposterous. We had to find something different and 'Change UK' as a concept came along. I was keen on it and it was actually quite a strong brand. We decided to register that, but the timing rules meant that we were barred from standing in the local elections. We could only stand in the European election. All because of the rules of the Electoral Commission.

The Liberal Democrats, however, were able to stand in the local elections, and they very cleverly recognised that if they could be perceived to perform well, if they could get people to vote in a local election about Brexit, with them as the protest party against Brexit, then they would be able to nix our strategy. They succeeded in that quite well, and I think they got up to the high teens. They turned around a fairly decent showing. It wasn't a brilliant performance, but it was spun by them as a massive comeback for the Liberal Democrats, which meant thereafter that, it was a quite a confusing picture, which a cynical Westminster lobby pounced upon. Should people vote Lib Dem if they were anti-Brexit? Should they vote for us if they were anti-Brexit? It was that issue, Brexit, that was cutting across what we were doing, which really did cause too many problems and too much turbulence in our development.

The European Elections

Mike Gapes: Events in Parliament meant a delay to Brexit. That meant that the UK would have to fight the May 23 European Parliament election. Our Independent Group had to make a quick decision. We could just about register for the European elections. We were all strong opponents of Brexit. And we felt we had to register as a party and fight those elections. However, I think the big mistake we made was that we hadn't factored in the impact of the boost that the Liberal Democrats would get from the local election campaign at the beginning of May. We were too late to register as a political party for the local government elections, and it would have been absurd to do so in any case. We had no infrastructure or membership. We were bystanders as the Lib Dems made gains from their very poor results four years earlier. The other thing we hadn't factored in was that when we were new and fresh and not a party, nobody saw us as a big threat to them. But once we'd actually made the decision to become a party, we were fair game for everyone. Tory, Labour, SNP, Plaid and especially Lib Dems all wanted to knock us down. The Liberal Democrats set out to kill us. They will deny it, but the reality is clear. Vince Cable falsely claimed that he'd offered us an electoral alliance, which would have been impossible under the D'Hondt closed list PR electoral system for the European Parliament. The Liberals and the Greens were both running full lists which they had already registered. They would have had to de-register themselves and then agree a different joint pro-European list of candidates in each region, and an alternative party name and registration at the Electoral Commission. The Greens had already ruled-out any joint list with the Lib Dems in November 2018. There was no way the Liberals and the Greens would have been able to run a joint list. So, a joint pro-EU list was a total non-starter, and Vince Cable knew it.

Mike Gapes: We had 3,700 applicants for candidates, and we spent the whole of Good Friday, Easter Saturday and Sunday in a conference centre at Kings Cross, interviewing people either by Skype or by phone or in person, to whittle down and determine a list of 70. We employed a firm to do checks of social media posts, but a couple of names got through that shouldn't have done and it was unfortunate and embarrassing. And, of course, our opponents and the media made a great fuss of that.

Chris Leslie: Over the Easter weekend we had to rapidly get candidates in place for the European elections. A tidal wave of 3,500 people applied to be candidates. It was a massive exercise. Basically, Anna Soubry and I had to do the heavy lifting of organising a process for interviewing and selecting people. It was really difficult. Chuka had gone on holiday, and his team stepped back too at that point, and in some ways that was the moment a simmering undercurrent of difficulties grew within our number. Luciana had gone off on maternity leave in February, so she wasn't overtly part of what we were doing after that. Gavin Shuker had been talking to her quite a lot and Gavin wasn't really participating fully by that point, which was very frustrating. It's still not clear to me what was really happening there. There was a difficulty when Gavin started to withdraw from the active side of work that Chuka and I, and Anna were organising for various, quite small administrative reasons, actually, looking back. I don't think he got his way on a couple of constitutional issues – and then there was a bigger problem about our leadership.

Anna Soubry: Well, we never really got the opportunity, because the European elections came along and that's what done us in. There is no debate that it would have been different if they hadn't come along when they did. The idea that we wouldn't stand candidates was never voiced in my hearing for sure. If we hadn't, can you imagine the response? You formed a new political party, and you have an opportunity and it's the central issue of the day and, indeed, of your party, effectively, in many ways, and you're not standing. I mean, how could we not have stood? Unfortunately, it did expose the naivety and lack of experience of a number of key people.

Leadership Issues

Mike Gapes: Another issue we had to address was our leadership. Initially, in February, we had all agreed that as we were not a political party, were going to have a collective leadership. We were going to work things out gradually. We had to have a spokesperson for the media, and Chuka was the obvious person for that and he was appointed, but we deliberately didn't have a leader. We had a convener for our meetings and organisation, which Gavin Shuker did. However, the Electoral Commission insisted, if you're going to be a registered political party, to fight the European elections, you're going to have to have a named leader. We couldn't have two leaders, we tried, they wouldn't have it. So, we had to have one named leader. It became very clear that, although the logical thing would have been that Chuka be the leader, a minority of our group including Luciana Berger and Angela Smith were strongly opposed to naming Chuka Umunna as the leader, even on an interim basis. When push came to shove, Chuka stood down and wouldn't do it, even though there was a clear majority for him. He was still the spokesperson, but Heidi Allen was put in as the interim leader. To be fair to Heidi, she said herself that she was very inexperienced, and, unfortunately, during the European campaign, that became very clear.

Chris Leslie: It seemed very natural to me that Chuka was probably the most media-visible person and should have been our leader from the get-go. We didn't necessarily want to have to pick a leader, but the Electoral Commission (them again!) insisted; if you're a party, you have to have a name that they approve of, and you have to have a leader. There were no two ways about it. We knew we had to pick a leader and that was where other difficulties started. Luciana, and I still don't quite understand why, adamantly vetoed Chuka as the leader, from a distance by conference call. She wasn't in the meetings, so we never really quite understood why. It was partly explained second-hand via Gavin that maybe Chuka would deter other Labour MPs from leaving the PLP and join us. It didn't really feel as though that was a particularly strong reason, but there was always a threat that if we didn't go along with that point of view, then she would then leave us, and we felt that Luciana leaving the Independent Group would be disastrous and therefore, we had to acquiesce with her, with her veto of Chuka. That caused some bad blood, unfortunately. Although Chuka was quite gracious in stepping back at Luciana's insistence.

After Chuka couldn't be the leader, we had to think, *"Well, who can we have that will be sufficiently interesting and charismatic on the media?"* We decided Heidi Allen was probably somebody who would have a different perspective and would be able to voice things in a certain way because it was very much about Brexit. Again, in retrospect, that was an error, because although she had good, very strong emotional intelligence, she didn't really have any political experience and was quite easily swayed by those who managed to get in front of her. There was a period before we stood where a number of Liberal Democrats, from the House of Lords, and business donors, had met Heidi and persuaded her that really Change UK should stand aside for the Liberal Democrats; that concept was just was planted in her mind, and started to eat away at her and obviously, we didn't agree with that, because we were fighting for our own viability. And if the LibDems were ever the solution to British politics we'd have seen it by then! But that situation worsened, and that conversation from her got increasingly tangled, and because she was the leader, even though we met as a management council, we had to implore her, "Look, we're in this business, let's fight, let's do our best around the country." We held a series of rallies across the country, but she became less keen to attend them.

Chris Leslie: Other MPs, including Gavin, didn't want to attend most of our European election rallies and it was just confusion and disagreement, which just worsened and worsened, to a point where Anna and I then learned that Heidi was going to go on Channel 4 News, just days before polling day, and announce to the country that she was urging people to vote Liberal Democrat in certain parts of the country! It was a complete and utter disaster. How would you get people to vote for Change UK in London when you were telling them to vote Liberal Democrat elsewhere? It was ridiculous, and unfortunately, once the leadership was in that position, we found ourselves internally having to firefight our way through it day-by-day. It was incredibly stressful. We would have daily telephone conference calls, which didn't resolve particularly well, and ultimately half of our MPs either lost their enthusiasm in that election or were probably nobbled by the LibDems; that was the sad story of heading towards that European election.

Election Results

Chris Leslie: The result actually wasn't a complete failure. We got less than a 4% of the vote, or around that amount, but there were still 600,000 votes across the country for us, and I think if we'd have stuck to a more distinct differentiated message from the old parties, from the Lib Dems in particular, it wouldn't necessarily have been irretrievable. We should have had a leader who understood the importance of lowering expectations and selling those wider values about the centre ground and changing politics, rather than becoming a pure anti-Brexit party at risk of being gazumped by the LibDems. I think we could have performed far better. We raised a lot of money and did a massive amount of work on that. I think we raised up to a million pounds, a lot of which was spent on social media. We hired some amazing staff, and they did their best, but it was a really difficult time. Particularly after the European elections, it was quite clear that some of our number were thinking about how they were going to survive in politics, and that's where the conversations that some of them had been having with the Liberal Democrats started to turn into reality; they were going to join the Lib Dems. Some very difficult meetings followed in the next few days, about how we should wrap it up and pull the plug on the whole thing.

Mike Gapes: The Lib Dems pulled a number of tricks against us. These included a press release claiming that former Tory MEP Julie Girling had left us to join them, when she had never been chosen as one of our candidates. They also got the head of our selected list of candidates in Scotland to participate in our conference call on a Sunday night and then on the Monday morning, announce that he was voting for the Lib Dems. Several of us, including Chris and Anna, wanted Chuka as spokesperson to push back against the Lib Dems, but he was always reluctant to do it.

Our analysis, and this was, ironically, written in an internal paper by Chuka in February, which was later leaked to the media, was that the Lib Dems were a significant part of the problem of British politics being broken. It wasn't just the two bigger parties; it was also the Liberal Democrats who were part of that tribal culture that we needed to end.

Naming Issues

Mike Gapes: There was an immediate issue to resolve issue about our name. We couldn't register as we Independents, according to the Electoral Commission, nor as the Independent Group. We had to be Change UK - the Independent Group. We faced threats of legal action from an American petitions website, and resolved them by an agreement that we'd change our name again after the election. We had tried to use a hashtag in our logo, in our brand, but our logo was rejected, by the Electoral Commission, so we then had to, in just a couple of days, produce an alternative logo, which wasn't perfect, but we didn't have time to test it. We were then ridiculed by the media for that logo. Everything was so pressured.

Chris Leslie: The other little side issue that was not known about during the European elections, but subsequently came to light, was that each of us were being threatened, personally, with being sued by an American petitions' website. They were sending us legal letters saying that unless we altered our party name we would be sued, because they claimed that by using the word 'Change' we were passing ourselves off as them. A couple of our group were frightened at the prospect of legal action, and so the majority view was that we had to settle with them. You can imagine the discussion we had about this. The problem was that we'd got into this culture that every decision had to be unanimous across the 11 MPs, and if one person said, "I'm vetoing the Leader," or, "I'm vetoing these photographs in this leaflet," or whatever, or "I'm leaving", then that was that. It became very fractious like that. When you're being threatened with being sued, of course, all it takes is one or two of you to say, "*Actually, no, I really think we have to take this seriously. My wife doesn't want me to go into a court case with our house potentially on the line,*" and so that was the case. The rest of us had to go along with acquiescing and an amicable legal agreement was reached. Chuka led on this mostly, and it finally involved an agreement where we managed to get them to say, "*Look, you know, we'll go through the European elections as 'Change UK,' but thereafter we will alter our name to something that was more suitable to them*". That meant we staved off the prospect of legal action against us for a few weeks until June.

Chris Leslie: One option was "Independent Group for Change" which I thought that was ridiculous, and embarrassing, but we just had to get through those European elections, and it was generally felt that we'd deal with that problem on the other side. When we got to the other side of course things were worse; we could see half of our MPs were going to leave, and they'd probably join the Lib Dems, and then we had this other problem that in a matter of weeks we were legally required to change our name. This was, if you remember, partly the responsibility of those ridiculously rigid rules that the Electoral Commission had set down. We were getting close to checkmate, and almost out of sheer determination and pride as much as anything else, those of us who'd been in politics slightly longer, myself, for 30 years, Ann Coffey and Mike obviously for 40 years, Anna Soubry and Joan Ryan; we were battle-hardened and I think we felt, "*Look, come on, stick together. Don't just disappear at the first hurdle. There are bigger, deeper things going on in politics, even beyond Brexit. It's not just about that.*" The others, who were slightly newer to politics, thought, I think, feeling that it was all about Brexit. They decided to put their eggs in the basket of the Lib Dems, and, as it turned out, that also proved to be a loser for them, because when it came to the general election in December 2019, indeed it wasn't all about Brexit, it was also about the state of Corbyn, and the alternative, and why Labour was un-electable. A lot of the electorate thought that they couldn't risk voting Lib Dem, if it meant Corbyn would come into office and hence, they moved and chose to vote Conservative rather than Liberal Democrat. None of them were re-elected.

Mike Gapes: But we'd supressed our vote by our own mistakes. Ideally, in retrospect, if we were to fight those elections in May 2019, I think we should have set up the Party with infrastructure by September or October 2018. That of course was not possible. No one knew in the Autumn of 2018 that the UK would be fighting those European elections. Ideally, we should not have done it just before the May local elections where we could not put up candidates. If we were going to establish a new party, we should have either done it in 2018, or we should have waited until well a after the local elections in May and then moved. But politics is not like that.

I recall my daughter had a book, by Lemony Snicket, "A Series of Unfortunate Events". Change UK was a bit like that. But personally, I would still do it again. When I left the Labour Party, people said I looked ten years younger. I looked like a weight had been lifted from me. The constant agonising every day, was over. I don't regret that.

I was very busy in the campaign. I spoke at meetings in Bristol, Canterbury, Birmingham, London, Nottingham, Manchester and Liverpool. We were operating on a shoestring with only limited support, but I enjoyed the campaign. But it was all to end in tears. In the last few days, Heidi Allen as our Leader had a series of media appearances in which she made a number of statements on television, and the radio, despite being told not to do so, calling for people to vote tactically for the Green Party or the Liberal Democrats in regions where they were better placed than we were. Several of us were furious at this. I thought it was treacherous stupidity. It was absolutely guaranteed to suppress our vote. Our best appeal was to moderate Labour and moderate Conservative voters who for good reasons did not want to vote Lib Dem. We had to be a credible choice for them. There was a big space on the centre left and centre right and if we were to build a new force in British politics, we had to get a hearing. We were fighting a regional list election where we had to get a quota to win a seat. We had hopes of winning one of the eight MEPs in London and one of the ten in the South East of England. But calling for votes for other parties helped to make that impossible. In retrospect I believe Heidi was already flirting with, and talking to Jo Swinson about future cooperation with the Lib Dems.

I came back from our final rally in Manchester two days before polling day on a late, delayed train to London. I was sitting with Chuka. He was really down. He said to me, "We can't do this." And I then knew the way that he was thinking and how things might go.

When the results were announced on Sunday evening it was clear that we had not done as well as we had hoped. Change UK got almost 600,000 votes, we only got 3.4% of the vote. In London we got 5% but we needed between 7% and 8%, to get Gavin Esler elected, and that was very disappointing and probably a game changer for us.

CHAPTER EIGHT

Post-Election Post-Mortem and Splits

"We were just a group of five of us in the end, basically standing on the matter of principle"

Mike Gapes: After the divisions in the campaign, it was clear that we needed an early post-mortem meeting. We met on 29 May in Sarah Wollaston's large Commons office. Our staff members Harry Burns and Nicola Murphy, and Chris Leslie as Campaign Manager gave honest, comprehensive reports. I thanked our team for their hard work but was very critical of the way that Heidi had gone off-message in the last few days. It was clear that we were fundamentally divided about the future. Six (Heidi, Chuka, Gavin, Angela, Luciana and Sarah) thought it was too difficult, and wished to close the party down and go back to being Independents, and five of us, Anna, Joan, Chris, Ann and myself said, *"No, we want to carry on."* After a frank exchange, we agreed to reconvene the following Tuesday, where we amicably, relatively, agreed that five of us would carry on and the others would leave.

Mike Gapes: At that time, the understanding was that all six of them were going to become Independents, but within two weeks, on 14 June, Chuka announced that he had joined the Lib Dems. He was followed by Sarah Wollaston in August, Luciana Berger in September and then later by Angela Smith and Heidi Allen. Only Gavin Shuker remained as an Independent MP.

When I left the Labour Party, I had to leave my Ilford Labour Party owned office, and find new rented premises, I also lost my two constituency staff, Sam and Rob, who were both politically active young men who made the decision to stay with the Labour Party. My two House of Commons staff, Daksha and Fiona, were older and not politically active. They had both worked with me for many years. They both decided to stay with me. I recruited two young constituents, Jack and Grace, to work in my new Ilford office. They were both outstanding.

Five Remain

Anna Soubry, Ann Coffey, Chris Leslie, Joan Ryan and
Mike Gapes outside the Houses of Parliament

Chris Leslie: We knew in the summer of 2019 that it was
pretty hopeless for us. We were just a group of
five of us in the end, basically standing on the

matter of principle, really. Four of us had left the Labour Party because we didn't agree with its values. Personally, I didn't think that I could suddenly become a Liberal Democrat, because I wasn't a Liberal Democrat, you know! I had different views to them on crime, and law and order, their drugs policy, international issues; they had a different political philosophy, and I didn't believe that I could just put all those views to one side. We survived with our integrity, but, obviously, not with many votes, because we weren't big enough. We weren't big enough to be known about. Three of us stood in the 2019 election in the end, me and Anna and Mike (Joan and Ann had decided to retire), and we fought to the end.

Anna Soubry: Joan and I were the only two with marginal seats and we work differently to colleagues in a safe seat. The relationship I had with my constituents and the way that I worked was very, very different. I'd like to think that I knew everything that was going on in my constituency, which is great because it means you can really get involved with individual cases and issues and really make a difference.

While I was an MP, I saw things and thought, *"God, if that was my constituent, that wouldn't be bloody happening; I'd have sorted that one out"*. I wouldn't grandstand and say, *"the system is useless and let's campaign against it"* my approach would be to get on the phone *"Right, I need food, I need medicines, I need this, I need that and the other. I'm going to put some money in. Will you get somebody else to help? Could you just give this?"* You know, you just do it. And these are things you don't – you never hear really about – but you'd do stuff like that all the time. And then, you'd be fighting the battle to get them their benefit or whatever the problem was sorted out. But you'd do real, real groundwork as well, and that was hugely rewarding, 'cause you do have power, as the MP, to do that.

Theresa May goes and is replaced by Boris Johnson

Mike Gapes: Theresa May resigned as PM, and Boris Johnson was elected by Tory members in July. He immediately began a divisive polarising strategy of confrontation with Parliament. After our party had split and the five had joined the Lib Dems, we were inevitably a less influential group in Parliament. I voted against an early general election, not for personal reasons, but because I wanted to hang Boris Johnson out to dry and try and get a better form of Brexit, to force him to a softer position. However, the stupid and the gullible and the ambitious combined together, as Corbyn and Swinson and Sturgeon created the majority Johnson needed to overturn the Fixed Term Parliament Act. I'm proud to say I was one of the MPs who voted against an early election at all stages, but I was in a very small minority.

Fighting On

Mike Gapes: Chris Leslie, Anna Soubry and I all decided we had to fight the election as Independent Group for Change candidates in our own constituencies. Joan Ryan and Ann Coffey decided to retire. I always knew I was on a kamikaze mission. We had no data or canvass records. They were all held by the Labour Party. I had no local party machine. But we fought a vigorous campaign ably co-ordinated by a great young agent, Jack Baldan, who had started work in June as one of my two new constituency caseworkers. Both Joan and Ann gave me vital support. I was assisted with deliveries by several local volunteers, and behind the scenes by a few prominent Labour members who were angry at the way their candidate selection had been stitched up by the Party Head Office for Momentum Corbynite "Stitch Up Sam" Tarry, after the local favourite, Council leader Jas Athwal, was suspended the night before the selection meeting. I also had help from Independent Group and Remain activists from elsewhere. We rented a large room upstairs at Ilford Catholic Club on the High Road. We gave Corbyn's candidate a good fight. My slogan was "Real Labour Values, and An Independent Mind". Corbyn Labour were furious. They even threatened legal action against us because we were using New Labour Red and Yellow as the colours of our leaflets. I pointed out that the Corbyn Labour colour was Dull Red not Bright Red and Yellow. Over a six-week campaign, I walked hundreds of thousands of steps and had thousands of warm, positive conversations, on doorsteps, on the street, outside schools, and stations. Many people came up to me to thank me for help I had given to them personally over the years. Despite the cold and dark, I enjoyed the campaign. At times I felt a bit like an ageing rock star on his final valedictory tour. In the end, of course, it was never going to be enough. I am sure I could have got a much higher vote than I did, but there was a definite hardening and polarisation in the last week. I was noticing people saying to me, "But if I vote for you, won't I let the Conservative in?" And I was saying, "Look, the Tories got 20% at the last election, I got 76%, so there is no way the Conservatives will win in Ilford South, you can safely vote for me without any danger of the Conservatives winning." But I suspect a lot of people had a different view.

Election Results

Mike Gapes: The Labour share of the vote was down 10.2% to 65.64%, and I got 3,891 almost 4,000 votes, 7.35%, and kept my deposit, but it wasn't anywhere near what I had hoped. I needed to both win Labour votes and squeeze the Tories to have any chance of second place. But the Tories had a good candidate, and the Tory vote was not squeezed at all, it was a very firm Brexit vote. Although Corbyn's candidate had won in Ilford South, and Wes Streeting was re-elected in Ilford North, Labour overall had its worst result since 1935, worse even than when I had fought and lost my first general election, in Ilford North in 1983.

The Lib Dems also fought a terrible campaign. The hubristic ambition of Jo Swinson was ended when she lost her seat as they got the result that they never expected.

The SNP had a result which was not quite as good as they'd hoped for, but they always prefer a Tory government to a Labour one. Labour was absolutely smashed because of the stupidity and the toxicity of Jeremy Corbyn. Many Labour MPs went into an election where they knew Corbyn was going to take them down. Some had expected that in 2017 too, but unexpectedly had survived. But this time he wasn't up against the incompetent Theresa May, he was up against the absolutely ruthless, cynical Boris Johnson. Some very good younger MPs lost their seats, and some who survived, including my neighbour Wes Streeting, are now on Keir Starmer's front bench.

Anna Soubry: One of the things that I have realised since is that the only people left of the group are the old timers. Of the remaining five, I am the one with the least Parliamentary experience. Chris, Ann, Joan and Mike have many more years as MPs under their belts. I was elected in 2010, Chuka Umunna 2010, Gavin Shuker 2010. Sarah Wollaston has never been involved in politics until she became an MP, and it was pretty much the same for Heidi Allen. Luciana was elected in 2010. Angela Smith in 2005. Compare some of their experience or rather lack of it to say Joan Ryan or Mike Gapes. Or Ann Coffey or Chris Leslie! We are also much the same age except Chris, who's younger. Chris was elected at the age of 24, and at the time, the Baby of the House. I'd also been around and had a job as a criminal barrister; I had a very different life to the others. I gave that up to become a Member of Parliament because I wanted to make a change and I wanted to make a difference. I often would say, obviously to a very discrete number of old friends, *"Bloody hell, you know, I gave that up for this."* "This" turned into being called a "Fucking Nazi" and chased down streets and all the rest of it.

Mike Gapes: All three of our Independent Group for Change MPs, Chris, Anna and myself, were defeated.

Dissolving the Party

Mike Gapes: After the election, we then had our discussions and we decided, collectively, that the party, The Independent Group for Change could not be sustained, we couldn't go on with no elected representatives. If we'd have won MEPs, then lots of things might have been different. If we had not had a general election in December, things might have been different; and if some more Labour MPs had joined us in February 2019, or if others had left the Labour Party after February who knows? But events did not work out that way.

CHAPTER NINE

Lessons Learned, Our Values and the Future – Some Final Thoughts

"Do you take a stand?"

Chris Leslie: At the end of the day, the question for me was, *"Do you take a stand, or do you stay silent, and let other people do the heavy lifting?"* I've always felt a heavy responsibility; when you're a Member of Parliament you're not there for your own aggrandisement, you're supposed to actually do what's right for the country. I felt that I had to do something and take a stand. I had hoped in those first three years or so after Corbyn became leader that we could we deal with the situation through "Plan A", bringing the membership to its senses, through shaking the tree in a way that would be resolved without personally sacrificing myself, but in the end, it did require sacrifice, and that is the story. It is a story of sacrifice in many ways, although I haven't personally been hurt in that sense; it's just career in Parliament that's gone as a result. I exchanged that for protecting the country from a hard-left ideology that I didn't think was right, and I think that was a price definitely well worth paying. I'm not saying it was a single-handed thing by any means, and I'm glad there was a group of many of us who believed that it was worth doing. It was very much driven by values, and what was right for the country and not by some tactical, short-term consideration.

Anna Soubry: I don't have any difficulty with this because I don't have a mortgage to pay, but, you know, Chris Leslie, he bloody does. And Chris Leslie is young, hugely talented, I mean so talented. At the moment he has little, if any, prospect of being back in politics and we need people like Chris Leslie in politics; that man's courage and sacrifice is outstanding. It's different for me and Mike and Ann. Chris was Shadow Chancellor at one point. If he'd kept his trap shut and had not been brave but kept quiet like the others, just think what position he would have in Starmer's Shadow Cabinet. He didn't; he did the right thing.

I could have stayed and fought and that was part of the discussions that I had with Nicky Morgan, for example, whether to stay and fight, or whether the party was beyond, not repair, but beyond hope of getting back to the centre. Actually, it wasn't just that, it wasn't just about the Conservative Party, it was actually that all of British politics was broken and that we needed to do things differently. I look at other Conservative colleagues who'd flirted with the idea of leaving, but it was too much a part their DNA, so if they'd left the Tory Party, they would have shed tears.

Mike Gapes: What does this all mean for me personally? I did say in an interview at the time that what we did in February 2019 might just be a small footnote in history. It will certainly be used by some people to say, well, you can't possibly try and break the party mould in the UK.

No Regrets

Chris Leslie: I don't regret leaving the Labour Party. I think the main aim of shining a spotlight on the problem was worth doing. It was worth having a shot at realigning British politics, but I think Brexit made that just too difficult to co-ordinate. Thankfully, the Labour Party has moved on, because it was defeated so heavily in December 2019, which I think was necessary for Labour, because it jolted them into getting rid of Corbyn and his gang. We definitely helped to contribute to that, and it was important that somebody did it. Had we not done what we'd done in February 2019, it's not entirely implausible to me that Corbyn couldn't have done again, perhaps with more success, what he did in the 2017 election. It was necessary for us to do what we did, and hopefully, in the longer run, the Labour Party will become more professional, progressive, and centre-grounded. The jury's still out as to whether they're in the position to do it because they still have a constitution where the members run the party, which is a difficult place to be.

Mike Gapes: By changing the terms of the debate, and pointing out the truth, we helped ensure that Corbyn did not win power. As I said at my election count after the result was announced,

I could not stand as Labour again because
Jeremy Corbyn is unfit to be Prime Minister.
I'm glad the British people agree with me.
Having said that, I didn't want Johnson to be
Prime Minister either. It was a terrible dilemma
for millions of voters.

Learning from History

Chris Leslie: History does, to a certain extent, repeat itself.
The parallels between what happened in the
Labour Party in the 1980s with Michael Foot
and Tony Benn came around full circle with
Corbyn and McDonnell. I would argue far
more damaging this more recent time around.
The lesson for me is crystal clear; progressives
must never lose sight of mainstream public
opinion, and the hard left cannot foist
ideologically extreme positions on the country
by hijacking what should normally be a
mainstream party. The self-regarding hard left
and moralism of identity politics will be
rejected by the public as it was so clearly in
2019 – and if those who genuinely seek to
govern for Labour as a mainstream party don't
grasp this nettle and pull it out from its roots,
the right-wing Conservative tradition will
continually be able to point to real dangers of
those views gaining a foothold in government.

Some voters – perhaps unfamiliar with this
political history – can be seduced by the
populism of neo-Marxism with its simplistic
black-and-white analysis and anti-capitalist
solutions. It can be quite comforting to believe
that all the world's problems lie at the door of

evil exploitative profit-seeking. In reality, the world is far more complicated and messier than this – and history is littered with the failed experiments of regimes corrupted by allocating resources and asset distribution through central state diktat. Social democracy is a distinct political philosophy from the Marxist traditions that infiltrated Labour in 2015. It took four years before they began to be disentangled again. The public must demand a credible alternative government to the Conservatives, and that must be from the social democratic tradition that itself rejects divisive dogmatism and looks to build on the best of our country and reform our market economy, not overturn our whole society as we know it.

I've come to learn that we take so many of these ideas for granted and that our major political parties – both Labour and Conservatives with Brexit – are highly prone to being infiltrated and hijacked. Perhaps there are wider constitutional safeguards needed in our parliamentary system to ensure the voters have choices that go beyond those insisted upon by party activists. I've learned that in politics, not everything can be about achieving new and great things; sometimes it is also about preventing really bad things from happening. In my case, I knew that it would be bad for Britain if the hard left ascended to government having hijacked the Labour Party and nobody took action to change or stop that. In the end, preventing that involved sacrificing my own time in Parliament, but it was a price well worth paying, and I am thankful that

I joined forces with my other colleagues in their courage and determination to jolt British politics just when the alarm needed sounding and the public alerting to what was going on. We may not have succeeded in realigning the party-political 'offer', but for a short time we electrified the political discourse in Britain and together we forced the pace of change which, because of the passivity of most others in Parliament, may not have otherwise occurred. The actions of a small number of individuals can help change the course of politics – and I am proud to have played my part in taking a stand when it mattered.

British Politics Is Broken

Anna Soubry: It wasn't just about changing the Tory Party. I understand the arguments, one of the big criticisms that could be made of me and my wonderful four remaining colleagues is whether we should have stayed and fought off our foes in our respective parties. There will be those who now sit in the Shadow Cabinet, or in amongst the Shadow Ministerial Team, who stayed. Whether they fought is another matter, but they stayed, and at the moment it looks like under Keir Starmer's leadership they are beginning to get their party back. I understand that, but that's for them. But that change in Labour only came about because they left. I believe subsequent events in the Tory Party have proved it was beyond redemption – the forces of darkness won Brexit, and there is no place never mind a platform for dissenters in the party.

I believe what we did was right and there is no debate about the fact that British politics is broken. In my opinion, there is no real debate going on at the moment. Whether Starmer can take the Labour Party to where it should be is debatable. He's a lawyer but whether he can make sure that things are now done on the basis of evidence and with courage and with principle, and whether he can shake away or get rid of the people who have poisoned the Labour well, remains to be seen. Personally, I can't see the Labour Party being that vehicle, but we can't go on as it is now.

Labour Values from Both Perspectives

Mike Gapes: I have still got, as I said on my election material, real Labour values, you cut me open and I'm still passionately Labour. I'm interested in Labour history still and I'm really interested in what's going on in the Labour Party now. I've still got loads of friends who are Labour people, and I'm talking to Labour MPs all the time, I have no intention of playing any frontline role in politics now. I certainly won't stand again. I think it's too early to say whether I would re-join the party. There is a rule in the Labour Party that if you are expelled, you are excluded for five years. I wasn't expelled, I resigned, I presume if I'd have just resigned, I could potentially just re-join, but I didn't just resign, I stood against Labour at an election. I'm not sure whether that five-year exclusion applies, or whether there is another form of exclusion or if it would need to be a special dispensation. I will not re-join the Labour

Party unless I'm welcome, and I'm not sure whether I would be welcomed at the moment. I think that depends on how successful Keir Starmer is in changing the Labour Party. Only time will tell.

Anna Soubry: I think it's quite interesting that my team, when I was a Member of Parliament, were not really involved in party politics at all. When they met my new colleagues and their teams, it was quite interesting because they were looked on with some suspicion because they thought they were "Tories". Whereas my lot never looked at them thinking, ooh, they're Labour. I think that showed a lot about our lack of tribalism, and while I understood it, I don't like it.

My team couldn't understand why members of my new colleagues' teams had actually shed tears when they left the Labour Party. They just found that extraordinary, whereas I understood why they did it, but none of us shed a tear, for God's sakes. I think if you're a member of the Labour Party it becomes much more all-consuming of your heart and soul, as well as your mind. It was their absolute life, in a way that it hadn't been for me and, to be fair, hadn't been for Sarah or Heidi.

"What Is Politics About?"

Ann Coffey: The Labour Party feels very much like the party of the last century, fighting old battles, looking back and not forward, and, like Lot's wife, being turned to salt. It needs to look forward with policies for the digital age which will impact on every aspect of our life. It needs a Harold Wilson "white heat of technology" moment.

One thing the Labour Party needs to recognise is to go on endlessly about how evil the' Tories' is not the path to power. I remember marching in the 80s to the chant of *"Maggie, Maggie, Maggie. Out, Out, Out"*. In every election in that decade the electorate said, *"Maggie, Maggie, Maggie. In, In, In."* We lamented the influence of the right-wing press and carried on convinced like the Jehovah's witnesses that our words would convince the voters if we could get a hearing. The lesson of the last election should have been learned in the 80s. Many felt Labour no longer represented their values and did not trust the party with Jeremy Corbyn as leader.

"Why Become an MP?"

Anna Soubry: When I didn't get re-elected, I was not an unhappy girl, I can assure you, because I often used to think, *"Crikey me, you know, I used to have a very nice life"*. That sounds terribly holier than though, but it is true. You know, you do look at some MPs and you think, blimey; I don't know why you're in politics, I don't know what motivates you. You do worry sometimes that you always say, *"All politicians want to make change and make a difference."* I do sometimes wonder. Sorry, I shouldn't say that, but, no, but it's true, though. There were some people, certainly in the Conservative benches, I can think of, who, if they want to change things, it was, you know, *"To get out of the European Union, stop immigration and, you know, get our country back,"* blah, blah, all this bollocks. But the idea that they wanted to be – you know, they had some greater view of things is not true. I can think of a number of them, they were just huge egotists and they just got off on being a Member of Parliament. You can see the whole way that they stand in the House of Commons and they conduct themselves. You know, ego, the power of the ego is enormous amongst many of them. I often used to think, I cannot tell you the number of times I used to think, *"You know what, I don't need this shit."* I just don't need it. I used to say, *"Do you know, I used to have a really great life?"* What I did get real satisfaction from was the constituency work.

Just to say that the danger in arguing for politicians to have more courage and principles is that you run the risk, (and it sounds like I'm just criticising the Blair government), but I think that there is a risk that you can create a political elite that loses its connection, its roots with the people it is meant to represent, as well as lead. I think that was a problem that had occurred through many governments and when we had the opportunity in 2010 to do things differently, we absolutely couldn't do it.

As I became a Member of Parliament, in my early years, I just knew there was this enormous disconnect, and I saw it as a minister as well, between what government thinks is happening and believes is happening, and what is actually happening. The total disconnect in terms of government policy that is not being actually done on the ground is also a disconnect between the way that politics happens and is also disconnected from the lives of real people. Too many politicians have lost contact with their constituents.

Anybody reading that would go, *"Oh, my God, what a hypocrite she is, because her constituents voted to leave the European Union"*; we all know all the stuff that I've been involved in in the last few years, but I never lost sight of the fact of what lots of my constituents were saying. I knew it was unpopular with large swathes of them, I knew that. I like to think it was part of the courage that I showed was that I was brave enough to say, I could take the easy route here and just go, *"My constituents voted to leave, that's it, end of. I'll just troop through the lobbies, keep my head down,"* like so many did. Instead, I said, *"I know, but I think you made a mistake. I'm not trying to stop Brexit, I'm simply saying, that I think we should have another look at it, guys, now we really know what it is and now we've got the deal."* And that was all it was, it wasn't about stopping it, it was about being, I think, courageous enough to say, *"I think we made a mistake. You know, you might not agree with me, but I think we should take it back and have another look at it."* That position stood in the face of what I knew a lot of my constituents did not agree with. That is the role of a politician: to try and make the case and be courageous and brave.

There's that famous quote by Erskine May, who wrote the Parliamentary bible that says that your Member of Parliament is a representative. None of us would ever put ourselves in the same league as Churchill, but who was the person who was consistently speaking truth to power and was not in line with public opinion, but was absolutely right about what was happening in Nazi Germany and the need to go to war?

Difficulties Forming a New Party

Ann Coffey: I think that one of the things that came out of my experience with Change was a reminder, yet again, of how difficult it is to form a new party in our current system. There may have been a moment of opportunity in February 2019 when we left. If a significant number of Labour MPs had left with us, I think we could have formed a new party with the Liberal Democrats who were struggling. They had the local organisation as well. We could have made gains in the local elections and as a new party in the European elections.

As a credible force for change, we could have offered the electorate an option that wasn't Jeremy Corbyn's Labour or Boris Johnson's Conservatives and changed the political landscape.

Re-joining the Labour Party?

Chris Leslie: I don't think that I could re-join the party at the moment. The core of the Labour Party is not even in the position where it was in the early days of Kinnock. There are some historic parallels; Kinnock knew that he had to grasp the nettle and challenge the demons in his party. That process has not properly started in the Labour Party. They've got to the stage where they're trying to professionalise their opposition to the government, asking questions more adeptly and forensically, scrutinising better, and that's an important step, but it's only one step. Starmer hasn't yet taken a stand on positions of his own. We know what he's against; he's against the government, but we don't really know what he's *for* yet. But things may change. During the Labour leadership election, Starmer said, in his 10 pledges, that he was going to continue with very much of the Corbyn agenda on mass nationalisation, and I think that he wanted a 'Prevention of Military Intervention Act', implying that going to the aid of those facing distress or persecution must be 'prevented'? There are some worrying things in that; if he can move away from some of these old, hard-left tropes, then eventually professionalise, that would be a good thing. It's certainly an improvement and the early signs are better; there are no Marxists in charge of the party any longer, but I don't quite think they realise the scale of the challenge and where the public are.

And it will take a lot for me to forget those who turned a blind eye to the risks of Corbyn and the hard left. Sure, the Corbyn period has passed and there is less incompetence and ideological hatred. And the new 'soft left' team are telling us they will repair the damage, possibly even distancing themselves from that time, maybe ask us to absolve them of their time supporting Corbyn's team. The problem is, every time those MPs faced a choice between Corbyn and the country's interests, they chose Corbyn. And they asked the country to vote Corbyn into Number 10. I find it hard not to remember their actions. So, for me, it will be really hard to trust them in the near term.

Mike Gapes: A lot of people who were with the Independent Group for Change, have re-joined the Labour Party to make sure that Corbyn's successor was not a Corbynista. I have friends who joined the Labour Party again to support Jess Phillips, but then when Jess wasn't standing, they switched their votes to Lisa Nandy or to Keir Starmer. Other friends who stayed with the Labour Party, and privately, were voting for me. They too voted for Starmer or Nandy.

Responses to Covid-19 – Personal and Political

Anna Soubry: Look at the new regulations about tracking, if somebody has tested positive and you're a contact, you have to self-isolate for 14 days, and they thought Alok Sharma had it and it was suddenly, "We can't function." These are your rules; how do you think real people are living, for God's sakes? And this then comes back to that point about the disconnect between you as a politician, making laws, determining policy, without understanding, actually, this is how it impacts on real human beings. The trouble is far too many politicians do not see themselves as part of the rest of the population. It never occurs to them to think, "How would I live my life now, if I abided by that policy, or how I'm impacted by that policy, or impacted by that piece of legislation?" That is a huge failing of British politics. This man is not able to work, and she's not able to work, and they can't claim any form of benefit. That's right, because that's what the law says, because they have got indefinite leave to remain, they have no recourse to public funds, but they didn't realise that.

The Future of The Conservative Party

Anna Soubry: My biggest regret was in not making the new party work and in not helping to fix British politics. Somebody said to me, "Why didn't you check out Chuka before you left the Tory Party and formed a new party with him?" However, I didn't leave the Tory Party and help form a new party because of Chuka. I can't say I regret not asking more questions, but I would still have left the Conservative Party. I can't say that I regret that because it wouldn't have made a difference. I think there were things that happened in 2018 and in my opinion, the summer of that year is when we could have changed the whole direction of Brexit. I was very well warned by somebody I'd never met before, who I met at a cricket match, who had been involved in the SDP. He said, "Good luck to you and all the rest, but you know you won't succeed because you'll never change the Liberals. Until the Liberals agree that they have to disband and be part of something new, you will not make the progress that we need to make in this country to change the way we do politics and build a radical centrist sensible party." He was right.

As people see what's happening in the Conservative Party and with this dreadful government, they will move away from it. In fact, they're already moving away from it; you can see that in the polling and the confidence that is drifting away from the Conservative Party, and the government, as it's trying to, somehow, cope with this crisis and is doing such a bad job of it. As Johnson continues to fail to get a proper grip on coronavirus and fails to admit his mistakes, he will inevitably be caught out, and the British people will see him for what he is. In time, I think people will say, "Hang on a moment, they've lied about coronavirus, you know, with the fake stats, and all the rest of it, and they've been incompetent." They will realise those are exactly the same people who lied to them about Brexit, because it's exactly the same. It's the same route of populism: lying, playing on prejudices and all the rest of it. It all comes from that root, and what you're seeing in their handling of the coronavirus are the manifestations of what's so rotten about their politics and their ideology.

We accepted that British politics was broken, and we accepted that this was one of the things that led to Brexit. Why did so many people feel totally unrepresented, feeling "left behind"? What were we doing wrong as politicians?

Policy Formation: a new way forward?

Ann Coffey: Obviously, Change got overtaken by events, so we did not really have time to develop our policy. I think that we were very aware of the shortcomings of trying to produce a manifesto shopping list, each with its own section and specific commitments. Of course, no policy can exist by itself. A policy commitment in one area can impact on the ability to deliver policy in another. Apart from the limitations of this approach in dealing with complex areas, it can sometimes lead to promising what turn out to be undeliverable policies. This further undermines public trust in the political system.

I hadn't really been involved in policy making while I was in the Labour Party, but I was responsible for co-ordinating policy development when we started Change UK. A lot of people came into Change with very strong and different views on policies. We had to find a way of having a policy discussion that wasn't simply over issues that people felt strongly for and against but initiated a more constructive way of thinking about issues. We talked a lot about working in this different way at the Change gatherings we had. We were trying to stimulate more interesting and different ways of looking at things. This is why we began to think about the idea of developing policies that reflected a person's lifetime experience: the birth of a child; a child at school; a young person at work or as a student; a young working adult; a person in middle age; then an older person at work and retired. That approach would also recognise the diverse needs people have and the different barriers to opportunity. We were trying to get a sense, not only of pulling policies together (environmental, health, employment, housing) that supported the individual at whatever time in their life, but also thinking about what that person might need to help them make a transition to the next stage in their life. Consideration would also be given of what the contribution should be of the individual, the family, the wider community and government towards achieving a good society from which everybody would benefit.

As part of developing this policy approach, we also thought it would be interesting to talk to people, not only about what they needed at that particular point in their life, but about what they might need 10 or 20 years later and also what would have benefitted them earlier in their life. Having this approach would help different generations to understand the different needs of other generations.

I think our way of approaching policy jolts people out of their policy silos, their "for and against" tick list. It is a person-centric policy, looking at a person's lifeline, their life pathway. It's a way of putting the person at the centre of the policy but also being able to place the needs of the individual in the context of the benefit of that to the wider community. Because what is provided in community support for a person must have some benefit to the wider community. Support for policies is higher where people see that wider benefit. It is about the individual's life, but it's also about community benefit. So, at every stage of that person's life thinking about the best way to support that person, the other question is, where does the community benefit come in at each stage? Obviously, the community benefit is very, very clear when it comes to educating young children, but there is a community benefit in making education free for older people, because if older people are engaged in interesting stimulating activities, they're likely to remain healthier longer, that's a community benefit, but they've also got something to contribute back, and that's a community benefit as well.

I think that it's important that people don't just have a binary choice. I suspect that at the last election, although a lot of people did positively vote Conservative, I'm sure that some people voted Conservative as the least of two bad choices, as they saw it. They did not vote Liberal Democrat because they didn't think there was any point. When people feel depressed by the binary choice that they're being offered and really feel there is no party representing their views, that's not good for democracy in the long run. It's just the same old choices and no great confidence in either of them. This idea of representative democracy is very difficult even though the House of Commons has changed over the years. We now have more women represented and more people from minority communities. However, they still sit as members of the traditional parties. That means that people are still being offered binary choices.

I think if we had some kind of electoral reform that gave smaller parties who are representing a range of values a chance of getting some Members of Parliament elected, that might work better in the 21st century, so that people might feel at least they've got a voice. I think a lot of people don't feel that they have at the moment; they're voting for a party that represents maybe 10% of what they think.

But I think that in itself, even if it came about, is not enough, we need a written constitution which has checks and balances to the power and authority of the Prime Minister and the Executive.

Even if that came about that's not enough, there has to be an understanding that government has to be with consent if democracy is to survive. It will only survive if everybody feels there is something for them. They may not get all they want but what they see is fair and inclusive of them. The challenge of doing that is huge, and it has to be done with people not by manifestos written to meet the agenda of interest groups within the political parties. And it has to start with listening to people. The alternative is to have a political system that seeks to exploit division and hatred and prejudice.

The constituency link is valued and gives clarity to representation. It also has its disadvantages, because, sometimes, doing your constituency work is a great deal more rewarding than sitting in a committee in

Parliament on a statutory instrument. Over the years, Members of Parliament have built up quite a lot of resources for constituency staff. Being an MP gets you a hearing everywhere and because you are heard, the constituent is heard. People are grateful for your help, and you do feel you have achieved some good. And, of course, issues that constituents bring to surgeries are invaluable in exposing injustice, enabling challenge and campaigning. MPs are heard, and for people, MPs give them that voice they haven't got and the importance of that shouldn't be underestimated. People always remember personal help that made a difference to their lives.

But the trust that exists at that level needs to be embedded into the political system.

People don't trust politicians or our institutions. The church's reputation has been damaged by protecting priests who sexually abused children, the banks have been damaged by bankers' behaviour, MPs by expenses. Where are the trusted institutions?

All of this enables populist leaders to exploit the lack of trust and offer solutions that feed the prejudice and promise solutions that create further division; so, it continues. Change needs to come from the bottom up, building on the trust that comes with a well-established local reputation.

Chris Leslie: There was an extraordinary moment in 2018 and 2019 when both Labour and the Tories were reaching new depths of dysfunctionality and distance from the mainstream of the British public. A new centre-ground party – reaching from the Labour social democrats through to centrist Conservatives – could have taken off, but for two major factors. First, Brexit was a major complexity whose crosscurrents blew unusually across the political spectrum and did not allow the singular focus on where the main parties were moving ideologically. This made it far harder, in fact near impossible, to forge the necessary alliances. Second, the LibDems were clearly the "bed blockers" of the centre ground and are still failing to confront their baggage and impediments to this day. I think that if Vince Cable had stayed on as LibDem leader, perhaps he would have been able to have the longer-term foresight to recognise that their tired brand, reputation and narrow appeal needed to go in favour of a wider realignment. But because he departed and sparked a leadership race, his putative successors turned inwards, appealing just to their own membership (as happens in all party internal contests!) and cemented their desire to kill off other realignment efforts, such as the nascent Change UK. Neither Jo Swinson nor Ed Davey were willing or able to do anything other than see our emergence as competition, hence the scramble to establish themselves as the 'true anti-Brexit' protest receptacle in those 2019 local elections, where they were already a registered party of long standing. The subsequent departure of MPs from Change UK to the LibDems reflected their success in smothering the realignment... but in the longer run that LibDem brand and style of their party was never going to break the mould.

Ann Coffey: I have always believed that it is our responsibility to provide a better future for our children. That value is strong and joins parents and carers of children in a common cause across all cultures and countries, though we may not agree on how to achieve that or what that better future looks like. We also believe in the importance of education and helping children develop the skills to meet the challenges of the future.

In my last months as an MP, I visited a primary school to see a project where children were using Google apps to learn new skills. Children were working in the classroom on developing a project on their individual laptops as a team. Each had tasks to do in the project, which involved them checking facts and finding examples to support the team project. The most important skill the children were learning was fact checking. So how do you check whether Mount Everest is 70 miles high? Or how do you check whether that the information about the amount of plastic in the oceans is right? How do you check that the information you find is not fake? A very necessary skill for every aspect of life looking to the future will be this ability to establish facts, including the trustworthiness of the source.

That investment in our children will determine how we use technology in the future for the common good. As responsible citizens, they in turn will provide a better future for their children.

The Disconnect Between Politicians and the Public

Anna Soubry: When I was a minister, the number of times I would go out and face this. You hear a politician on the radio, government ministers, saying, *"Well, we've put £50 million this issue, we've done that."*

The story I'll never forget was that when we refused to bail out the steelworks near Redcar; we talked about the £60 million that we were going to give to mitigate the profound effect it would have on Redcar. I had always liked the Chief Executive of the unitary authority there, a wonderful, excellent woman. What must have freaked people out was that I had her mobile phone number. I've never forgotten this, it was a Saturday when I rang her up and said, *"I'm just checking how's it going?"* She did something, which she obviously thought was not quite the done thing, but she told me, *"Well, actually, we've got a problem, because all the apprentices have been found new apprentices' places with other companies locally."* This was a fantastic achievement. She added, *"But we haven't got the money."* I said, *"What do you mean you haven't got the money?"* She said, *"Well, Business"* (the department I was number two in) *"they won't give us the money for it."* I said, *"What do you mean they won't give you the money? I thought you were meant to be in charge of this £60m fund, you know? You've got this committee."*

The people of Redcar had been promised £68 million; it's all a load of old bollocks, it's bollocks. They had been told that the money had been made available, but that they had to apply for it. She said, *"Well, you know, we've asked for this."* It was something like, I don't think it was even £1 million, and these were proper three-year apprenticeships. Local businesses, magnificently, had made sure every single apprentice had a place; you can imagine how invaluable this would have been. Business was refusing to hand over the money. I sent off an email, I won't tell you everybody that was involved in that email, but it went as high as it possibly could in government, saying, *"I am absolutely appalled that this money is being held up by our department, by Business. There was no good reason. They have found a place for every apprentice, but they need the funding to pay these apprentices and the businesses and we're not doing it."* I was told, *"Well, if they've got an apprentice, they should pay for it themselves."* I answered, *"Yeah, but if they could afford an apprentice, they would have already taken on a fucking apprentice."* Anyway, that was on the Saturday. On the Monday I had a full meeting in my office, where I was just appalled. I said, *"Why haven't you given them the money?"* *"Oh, we've got to go through this process."* *"No, you don't have to go through this process and that process. We've set up a committee, we go out on the radio and on the television telling people, 'Well we've given them all this money and whatever they want they can have, and they will make the decisions locally'."* I said, *"It's just not true, it's not happening."* And it ended up with me having a full-blown argument with my then Secretary of State, with me threatening all manner of dreadful things if this money wasn't made available by the end of the week; anyway, it was. It shouldn't be like that, should it?

That's why you get this disconnect, and that's why you get people who go on radio, and on the television and they'll say, *"We've done this."* And then you get the guy who comes on who says, *"Well, I'm a business and it's just not happening."* And real-life viewers, real-life people, are sitting at home saying, *"Well, somebody here is not telling the truth."* Some of that frustration and anger is a lot to do with what happened with Brexit; the left-behind feeling they're not really interested in you. It's all hype, it's all spin.

To me, the critical part of politics is creating change and actually delivering, in reality, on the policies, on the laws that you passed. It is part of that reconnection with the lives of real people, that you, apparently, as a politician, want to change for the better.

For me, there was always a sense that you should do the right thing. I think that it came from my parents. I'm from a very average, middle class, middle England family. Our circumstances changed because what my parents had hoped would be their life didn't work out for them, because my father lost his business. And so, I went to what became the local comprehensive in Worksop, it was a tough school with a large number of pupils whose fathers were miners. There was a lot of real poverty in some of those communities that we had as our intake and part of our catchment area. For me, that was a bit of an eye-opener.

The Conservative Party Now

If you look at the Conservative Party now, where the Remain side lost the referendum, and in the winning of the referendum, the Conservative Party, especially under Boris Johnson's leadership, is absolutely in the grip of an ideologically driven sect, which is right-wing, and often strangely Libertarian. It doesn't believe in rules and regulations, often; all the things that keep us safe and make sure that we have an economic system that does the right thing by people, because we control the excesses of capitalism and so on, and we look after people and protect them and so on and so forth. It's very different now. We have a Foreign Secretary and a Home Secretary who contributed to a book that, basically, said British workers were the laziest in the world, who believe in deregulation, who believe in a different way of doing things than we have ever really seen in our country. Thatcher bought into a lot of this and, certainly, many of the people around her did, but she was always tempered by the fact that she included people who didn't share that ideology, like the Ken Clarkes, Michael Heseltines, that tempered it and actually kept the Conservative Party in the centre and under the influence of the more sensible forces of Conservatism. With the election of Johnson and in the choice of the people that he has put into Cabinet and the way that he is conducting his government, there is no room for dissent, because these people now completely control the Conservative Party. Those who don't share their ideology have no place in government and I think they don't have any place, actually, in the Tory Party. When you look at who's left in Parliament, where are the sensibles? They're certainly not in government and they're muted on the back benches, or they're the Chairs of Select Committees. So, that's where, for example, Greg Clark is. Jeremy Hunt, who I have never considered a likely member of the Tory Reform Group which Ken heads up, is now seen as quite radical, which shows an enormous shift in the Tory Party to the right.

Anna Soubry with Michael Heseltine

I'm afraid that history is going to record the last few years in a very poor light, because, I think, we have lacked courage; I cannot tell you the number of times people, including government ministers, cabinet ministers, who had voted entirely differently to me came up to me and said, *"Well done, keep on going."* It is, it's appalling. The ones who said, *"I just think you're so brave,"* including a Labour MP who I like very, very much and admired. While I was sat with Chris Leslie, he came up to me when we knew that the election was coming, we knew what our fate was, and he came up to us. His eyes filled; he was welling up with tears. *"I just think you've been so brave, you've both been so brave."* He got re-elected, by the way, and is now a shadow minister.

Anti-Semitism and The EHRC Report

Joan Ryan: There is a price to pay for anti-Semitism, the British people delivered their verdict, and Labour suffered a catastrophic defeat. The lessons of his leadership must be learned: it is important to confront every instance of anti-Semitism and confront it from the beginning. Far-left leadership cannot be engaged with in the manner that one normally deals with those in politics with whom we disagree. It is crucial to develop a clear critique with red lines that you are not willing to compromise. You cannot fight anti-Semitism without fighting anti-Zionism. Anti-Semitism is a very real threat to free societies, to democracy, it is corrosive and spreads like a virus.

The EHRC's damning report has revealed the extent to which the Labour Party – under Jeremy Corbyn's leadership – had become infected with the scourge of anti-Jewish racism. It is disgraceful that a party founded on the principle of equality has become mired in bigotry and prejudice and that so many Jewish members had to suffer such appalling abuse. Never again should anti-Jewish racism be dismissed as a smear. The toxic culture within the party must be expunged. An independent complaints system is required to investigate and deal swiftly with all outstanding cases of anti-Semitism and the perpetrators thrown out of the party. The Labour Party's adoption of the IHRA's definition of anti-Semitism should be used as basis for action and education to address hate and discrimination. And the demonisation and singling out of Israel must end. The party needs to develop a more balanced policy towards the Middle East and the Israeli-Palestinian conflict. By taking these steps, the Labour Party can begin the process of restoring its tarnished reputation.

Ann Coffey: The personal is political, and every political act has a personal dimension. We have to take responsibility for the choices we make.

There is not a tidy end to our story; we have been part of the change and churn in politics. Parliament has moved on to new issues, and new MPs elected in 2019 are facing the same challenges that we did: how do you resolve the conflict between party loyalty and individual beliefs?

We live in uncertain times, and if our parliamentary democracy is to survive with public support, people need to feel that their values are represented and articulated in Parliament. If they do not feel that then disenchantment leads to anger and gives a space for extremism and populist leaders whose policies inevitably lead to a further fracturing of the consensus that must be the building block of democracies.

The five MPs actions are a challenge to a party system which instead of protecting against extremism can become the vehicle for it.

Lightning Source UK Ltd.
Milton Keynes UK
UKHW010722080421
381640UK00001B/29